HAYAO KAWAI

DREAMS, MYTHS AND FAIRY TALES
IN JAPAN

Hayao Kawai

Dreams, Myths and Fairy Tales in Japan

DAIMON

Acknowledgments

This book has grown out of five lectures which originally were delivered at the Eranos Conferences of 1983, 1984, 1985, 1986 and 1988 and published in the *Eranos Jahrbuch* Volumes 52-55 and 57. Their use as the basis for the present book is with the permission of the Eranos Foundation, Ascona, Switzerland.

I would like to express my gratitude to Mr. and Mrs. Rudolf Ritzema for their kind hospitality during my stays at the conferences. My special thanks are due to the persons I met there: James Hillman, Wolfgang Giegelich, David Miller, Robert Bosnak and Paul Kugler, and also to my son, Toshio. I greatly enjoyed our exchange of ideas which stimulated my thinking in all ways. I would like to thank Gerow and Sachiko Reace and Mark Uno in the states, who helped me to write the papers in English.

I extend my thanks to the following parties for their permission to reproduce the illustrations contained in this book: Yata-Temple, Urashima-Shrine, Shyoju-raigo-Temple and Prof. Toshihiko Izutsu.

I express my heartfelt thanks to the International Research Exchange Foundation for Japanese Studies in Kyoto for the financial help toward the publication of this book.

My deepest thanks are due to Dr. Robert Hinshaw, who planned this publication, and to Dr. James Gerald Donat for his work of editing the manuscript.

Hayao Kawai

ISBN 3-85630-544-0

Dreams, Myths and Fairy Tales in Japan by Hayao Kawai
© 1995 Daimon, Einsiedeln, Switzerland
This edition edited by James Gerald Donat

Contents

List of Illustrations

Introduction

This book consists of five lectures which were originally given at Eranos Conferences, Ascona, Switzerland, from 1983 to 1988. All are concerned with Japanese culture: Japanese dreams, myths, fairy tales, and medieval stories.

In my youth, I was strongly attracted to Western culture. With my experiences of the Second World War, I came to hate the irrational and constantly vague Japanese attitude toward life. Scientific rational thinking stood as the symbol of the West and always as a creative treasure for me to capture.

In 1959, I came to the United States to study clinical psychology in order to become like a Westerner. The experience in fact opened the way to Jung's psychology, by which I was able to find myself as a Japanese. After my initial years of study in the United States, I went to the C.G. Jung Institute in Zürich, Switzerland, receiving a diploma there in 1965. Interestingly, Western analysts helped me find the values of Japanese culture. Before that, I was of the opinion that the Japanese must make efforts to establish a modern ego, following the European way completely. Then all of the unique features of Japanese tradition seemed for me to be utterly disgusting and unbearable. The old ways of living had to be discarded as soon as possible. However, I began to realize, through my analytical experiences, that European consciousness is not "the best" nor "the only one" for everybody in the world to attain. Jung talked about the importance of Self to which the conscious ego must surrender. If Self is most precious there might be other ways to reach it, other than following the European way with its ego-Self axis.

If Self-realization is understood as a process and not a goal, we can compare the process for Japanese and Westerners, and benefit each other without concern for which is better or worse. Although I still retain my opinion that the Japanese must learn from the modern European way of ego establishment, they do not have to imitate it completely. The Japanese must struggle to find their own way. For my part, I began to investigate Japanese mythology, fairy tales, and old stories because they contain so much knowledge of the unconscious. They were first told by a consciousness which is different from the modern ego. Their features give us hints about the new conscious states of we modern Japanese. Westerners might be interested in these new states, if they too are trying to find a way to go beyond their own modern ego.

In the first chapter, some medieval stories are discussed, especially those having to do with dreams. At that time, the demarcation lines between conscious and unconscious and between human beings and Nature are very thin. With that kind of consciousness, one can certainly have a different view of the world from that of modern people. Medieval persons can acknowledge inner reality much more freely and easily.

The second chapter is about a Japanese priest in the 12th-13th Centuries called "Myôe," who keeps a dream diary until the end of his life. With interpretations of some of his dreams, I try to show how his state of consciousness is different from that of modern people. As a result of his dream experiences he claims to attain the state of "coagulation of body and mind." It is a hint for thinking about the difficult issue of the body and mind continuum. It is indeed a different approach from Descartes.

The third chapter deals with Japanese mythology. There I pay attention to gods who are neglected in the Japanese pantheon. The mightiest God is the center in

Christianity; a god who does nothing stands in the center of the Japanese pantheon. This remarkable difference is reflected in their psychology and ways of living.

In the fourth chapter, I discuss Japanese fairy tales in connection with the theme of beauty. Japanese fairy tales have a completely different structure from Grimm's tales. We seldom find a Japanese fairy tale in which a male hero attains the goal of marrying a beautiful woman after accomplishing the difficult tasks assigned to him. In this chapter, I try to make it clear that the main thrust of Japanese fairy tales is aesthetic rather than ethical. Japanese fairy tales convey to us what is beautiful instead of what is good.

In the last chapter, I discuss the long medieval story called "Torikaebaya." A boy is raised as a girl, and a girl, his sister, is raised as a boy. The girl herself pretends to be a boy, even eventually marrying a woman. With the exchange of sexual roles, the story implies that the clearcut division between manliness and womanliness is artificial. Human beings have rich possibilities – one can be manly and womanly at the same time. The story gives us suggestions to enrich our ways of life.

In these chapters I compare some characteristics of Japanese culture with those of the West. I am afraid readers may feel I put too much value on the Asian side. In fact I think both are equally important. Until recently I had thought in terms of integrating the two, or of finding a third way somewhere between them. But nowadays I think it is impossible. I now feel that we can be conscious of the state of being we are in and of the advantage and disadvantage of it in detail. It might be better if we could switch from one attitude to another according to the situation.

I shall be happy if this book in some way helps readers in the West see their own way of life from a different angle.

Figure 1. Jizô Bodisatva rescuing a person in Hell

I. Interpenetration:

Dreams in Medieval Japan

1. Dreams

A dream is a peculiar product. When I have a dream, I refer to it as my dream, but to whom does the dream really belong? I call a painting mine insofar as it is my creation with which I am free to do as I wish – I can keep it or destroy it. We do not make our dreams and yet we call them our own. To speak of a dream as being "mine" is somewhat like saying, "This is my Picasso." Although Picasso did the painting, I claim it as mine and can do with it as I please. However, there is a problem with this analogy. Where is the "Picasso" who painted my dream? Furthermore, I cannot control a dream as freely as a painting. Sometimes I even feel that a dream destroys me.

Perhaps it would be more appropriate to say that a dream is like a butterfly which happens to fly into my garden. I can see and appreciate it, but the butterfly comes and goes of its own accord. I can catch it and literally pin it down to analyze, but it would have undergone an important change, for then it would already be dead. Some of you may be familiar with the story of Chuang Tzu (ca. 330 B.C.) and the butterfly. Chuang Tzu once dreamt that he had become a butterfly. Upon awakening he wondered whether it was a human being who had just dreamt of being a butterfly, or a butterfly which had dreamt that it had become a human being. Chuang Tzu raises a big question: Can it be that my whole life is someone else's dream?

Most people today assume that their dreams belong to them, but do not feel responsible for what they dream. This contradictory attitude reveals a flaw in the prevalent understanding of dreams. I think it may be more accurate to say that they belong to the cosmos as well as to the human being who sees them.

In this respect people in pre-modern societies had a more suitable attitude towards their dreams. Before I explain what I mean by this, I would like to tell a story about dream experiences in medieval Japan. The following episode appears in the *Uji Shui Monogatari (USM)*, a collection of stories compiled at the beginning of the thirteenth century:

> There was a man living with his wife and only daughter. He loved his daughter very much and made several attempts to arrange a good marriage for her, but was unable to succeed. Hoping for better fortune he built a temple in his backyard, enshrined it with the bodhisattva of compassion, Kannon, and asked the deity to help his daughter. He died one day, followed by his wife shortly thereafter, and the daughter was left to herself. Though her parents had been wealthy she gradually became poor and eventually even the servants left.
>
> Utterly alone, she had a dream one night in which an old priest emerged from the temple of Kannon in the backyard and said to her, "Because I love you so much, I would like to arrange a marriage for you. A man I have called will visit here tomorrow. You should do whatever he asks." The next night a man with about thirty retainers came to her home. He seemed quite kind and proposed to marry her. He was attracted to her because she reminded him of his deceased wife. Remembering the words which Kannon had spoken to her in her dream, she accepted his proposal. The man was very pleased and told her that he would be back the next day after attending to some business.
>
> More than twenty of his retainers remained behind to

spend the night at her home. She wanted to be a good hostess and prepare a meal for them, but she was too poor to do so. Just then an unknown woman appeared who identified herself as the daughter of a servant who used to work for the parents of the hostess a long time ago. Sympathetic to the hostess' plight, she told the latter that she would bring food from her home to feed the guests. When the man returned the next day, she helped the daughter of her parents' master again by serving the man and his attendants. The hostess showed her gratitude by giving her helper a red ceremonial skirt (Jpn. *hakama*).

When the time came to depart with her fiancé, she went to the temple of Kannon to express her thanks. To her surprise she found the red skirt on the shoulder of the statue; she realized then that the woman who had come to help her was actually a manifestation of Kannon.[1]

In this story we see the free interpenetration of this world and the dream world, a common feature of medieval Japanese stories concerning dreams. What Kannon foretells in the dream is realized in the waking world, and the bodhisattva manifests himself in the form of an actual human being.

Before continuing I would like to say a little more about the sources which I am using. These are the *Uji Shui Monogatari*, which I mentioned earlier, and the *Myôe Shonin Yume no Ki*, or *The Dream Diary of Saint Myôe*.

During the Kamakura and Muromachi Periods in Japan several major collections of religious stories were compiled. The *USM is* one of these and contains anec-

---

1. *Uji Shui Monogatari*, revision and commentary by Etsuji Nakajima, Kadokawa Shoten, Tokyo, 1960, Ch. 9, No. 3 (108). I am giving somewhat shortened summaries of the original versions here. There is an English translation of the *USM: A Collection of Tales from Uji: A Study and Translation of the Uji Shui Monogatari*, trans. by D.E. Mills, Cambridge University Press, Cambridge, 1970. The corresponding episode number is in the parentheses.

dotes, legends, and records of historical events from India, China, and Japan which Buddhist priests used in their sermons. All strata of society are represented in these tales. Unknown members of the lower classes as well as famous warriors and nobles appear in them. It is difficult to say how and when they evolved; some have been transmitted down to this day in the form of fairy tales and are still being modified. Although they are primarily didactic Buddhist episodes, they are interesting from the standpoint of depth psychology due to the inclusion of dreams and fantasies. Many of them appear in variations or in virtually the same version in several different collections. I have chosen the *USM* because it contains many outstanding examples of the interpenetration of the dream and waking worlds. The period of its compilation overlaps with the life of Myôe (1173–1232) whose dreams I will also discuss.

2. Life and Death

The land of death is easily entered in the dreams of medieval Japan. The following is a typical example:

> There was a Buddhist priest named Chiin Kano who failed to keep the precepts and was only interested in worldly affairs. On the side of the road leading up to his temple there was a tower enshrined with an old neglected statue of the bodhisattva Jizo. Occasionally the priest would remove his hood and bow to the statue as he passed by.
>
> After he died, his master said, "That priest was always breaking the precepts. He was so bad he's surely gone to hell," but the master still felt sorry for him.
>
> Shortly thereafter, some people from the temple noticed that the statue of Jizo had disappeared from the tower and

thought that the statue might have been taken out for repair.

One night the master had a dream: A priest appeared and said, "Jizo has gone to hell with priest Chiin Kano in order to help him." The master then asked why Bodhisattva Jizo had gone to accompany such a bad priest. The priest in the dream replied, "Because Chiin Kano bowed to Jizo sometimes when he passed by the tower." Upon awakening, the master went to the tower to check for himself and saw that the statue of Jizo was actually gone

After a while he had another dream in which he went to the tower and found Jizo standing there. He asked why Jizo had reappeared, and a voice said, "Jizo has returned from hell, where he had gone to help Chiin Kano. The fire has burned his feet." Upon awakening, the master hurried to the tower and saw that Jizo's feet had actually been charred. He was deeply moved, and tears flowed down his face.

After hearing this story, many went to worship the statue of Jizo in the tower.[1]

Jizo went to hell and returned to this world with actual evidence of his journey. The circumstances surrounding his disappearance were all related in dreams. The *USM* contains numerous stories in which not only bodhisattvas but ordinary humans also go to and return from the land of death, and a large number of these involve dreams. Whether such stories are "real" is not our concern. What is important is that through them we can learn about the kind of cosmos the people of that period lived in.

What we have seen so far is that their cosmology included the land of death, or life after death. In order to really think about our lives I feel that it is important to take a standpoint which encompasses both this world and the next.

1. *USM*, Ch. 5, No. 13 (82).

Here is another story about a man who goes to the land of death:

There was a talented calligrapher named Toshiyuki, and some two hundred people asked him to copy the Lotus Sutra, an important Buddhist scripture. (It was customary during that time to have scriptures copied as a means of accruing merit towards an auspicious afterlife.)

One day Toshiyuki became mortally ill, and just as he thought, "I'm going to die," he was caught by an unknown man who took him to the land of death. There Toshiyuki saw two hundred horrible-looking people, all wearing armor and breathing fire from their mouths. Terrified, he asked his captor who these people were. The man told him that they were the ones who had asked Toshiyuki to copy the Lotus Sutra. They were now suffering unexpectedly because he had made the copies with defiled hands: he had failed to purify them after having relations with women or eating fish. Toshiyuki had not actually been fated to die, but was brought to the land of death to suffer revenge. His captor told him that his body would be cut into two hundred pieces, and his mind divided among them to experience the pain. They came to a river flowing with a thick, black liquid, and he was told that it was the ink which he had used to copy the sutra. The copies he had made had to be washed away because they were impure.

When he went before the court of the land of death, he vowed to copy the Suvarna-prabhâsa Sutra, a lengthy four-volume scripture, and he was allowed to return to this world. He made this vow because the man had told him that this was the only way to be rescued. Upon returning he felt that what he had just experienced "was like looking into a clear, bright mirror," and he was firmly resolved to copy the sutra. But when he became well again, he forgot about everything and spent his time pursuing women instead.

He died a few years later, and an acquaintance named Tomonori Kino had a dream about him: Toshiyuki looked so terrible that he was hardly recognizable. He told Tomonori,

"I came back to life with the help of my vow to copy sutras, but now I am suffering unbearably because I did not fulfill the vow. If you have any sympathy, please find the paper I had set aside for copying, take it to the monk at the temple of Miidera, and ask him to do what I had promised." The dream ended with Toshiyuki crying bitterly. As soon as he awoke he went to get the paper and took it to the monk at Miidera. The monk was glad to see him and said that Toshiyuki had appeared in a dream asking him to copy the sutra on the paper that Tomonori Kino brought.

The monk made the copies and held a service for Toshiyuki. He reappeared in the dreams of both Tomonori Kino and the monk of Miidera, and he looked much better.[1]

Although what he saw in the land of death did not help him change his earthly life, his experiences there clearly mirrored his life in this world. The remarkable synchronicity of events in dreams, this world, and the land of death was not considered unusual.

3. Which is the Real Reality?

As I was reading the stories in the *USM*, I began to feel the people of that time believed that reality had many layers, and that its appearance differed greatly according to the layer being seen. The next story illustrates this view of multiple realities:

There was a man who fell in love with the daughter of the priest of Daianji Temple in Nara. He was so attached to her that he would even sleep with her during the day. Once when he dozed off he saw the following dream: The people in the house suddenly started to cry, and he looked at them in surprise. The priest and his wife [i.e., the parents of the man's lover], the servants, and everyone else were drinking

1. *USM*, ch. 8, no. 4 (102).

molten copper from a large earthenware vessel. One of the servants called to the daughter who had been sleeping beside the man. She cried as she drank the scalding liquid from a silver bowl, and smoke came out of her eyes and nose. The servant then offered the bowl to the dreamer. He became frantic and awoke from the dream.

When he returned to the waking world, he was startled to find a servant bringing him food. He heard the sound of the family eating and thought, "They are recklessly consuming what belongs to the temple. That is what I saw [in the dream]." He was so disgusted that his feelings of affection for the daughter vanished without a trace. He declined the food, left the house, and never returned.[1]

In his dream the man sees a layer of reality different from that of external appearances. Without the view which the dream affords him, the family would seem to be simply enjoying a meal together. Because he feels the scene in which he saw them being tormented is closer to the truth, he decides to end his relationship with his lover and her family. Yet, on an entirely different level, one might say that without any good reason he lost his chance to establish himself in the rich priest's family.

It is an uncanny world in which an entire family drinks molten copper, but what the man sees is more representative of the truth, or in Jung's terms, of psychic reality.

The following story is even more uncanny and involves life after death. It is concerned with the father-son relationship and makes for an interesting comparison with the myth of Oedipus:

There was a Buddhist priest named Jokaku who lived near the temple of Kamitsuizumoji in northern Kyoto. He had succeeded to the temple following the death of his father, but it was now in a state of disrepair.

One day he had the following dream: His father appeared,

1. *USM,* Ch. 9, No. 7 (112).

looking very old and carrying a long stick in his hand. He said, "At two in the afternoon the day after tomorrow, this temple will be destroyed by a storm. I am now living as a big catfish in a puddle underneath. When the temple falls down, I shall appear in the garden. Please help me and set me free in the Kamo River." Upon awakening Jokaku told his family, and they wondered what the dream meant.

Two days later the temple collapsed in a great storm, and a large catfish swam up to Jokaku. Without a moment's thought he speared it with an iron rod and was quite pleased with his catch. He wanted to cook it, but his wife scolded him for killing the fish from his dream. He gave no heed and replied, "Father will be quite happy as long as no one except [his son] and grandsons eat him." He boiled the fish and ate it with his sons. "The reason this fish is so tasty must be that it's my father's flesh." Just then a big bone pierced his throat, and he later died in pain. His wife was so horrified that she never ate catfish again.[1]

In his dream Jokaku perceives another layer of reality. He is willing to believe that the catfish is his father, but fails to carry out its request and thus loses his life. In this respect I do not think he actually believes the dream, because for him that catfish's assertion about being his father seems to be nothing more than a joke. The theme of the story in terms of traditional morality is filial piety, but it can be given many interpretations from the standpoint of depth psychology. I find the following points to be particularly striking:

Eating is a primitive expression of identification, and eating the flesh of one's forbears is one example. We might expect that the son would transmit his father's soul by consuming the latter's flesh, but I have found no evidence for this in Japanese literature. In this story the father dies, and it is the grandson who transmits the grand-

1. *USM*, Ch. 13, No. 8 (168).

father's soul. The mother must live on to protect the grandchildren, and we thus have the triad of the mother, son, and the soul of the grandfather, an important constellation in the psychic life of the Japanese.

When this episode is compared with the myth of Oedipus, two important differences become apparent: First, although both Oedipus and the man in this story kill their fathers, the Japanese son is aware that he is killing his father whereas Oedipus only learned this after the fact. Second, the Japanese murder is motivated by the desire to eat and not by the desire for power or sex. The appetite for food is more connected to the body than the other two.

4. I and the Other

The relation between others and myself is very subtle. Although we may feel that you and I are clearly distinct, there are many interpenetrating components, especially in the dream world. The following story shows how this interpenetration manifested itself in the people of medieval Japan:

In the town of Tsukuma in Shinano Province there was a medicinal hot spring. A man living nearby had a dream in which a voice said to him, "At midday tomorrow the bodhisattva Kannon will come to the hot spring." The man asked how the deity would make his appearance, and the voice replied that a bearded warrior about thirty years old would come riding on a horse, and went on to describe his outfit and gear.

Upon awakening the man told some others about his dream, and many people gathered to clean the hot spring and decorate it with flowers. Around two in the afternoon a warrior fitting the description from the dream came riding on a horse. Everyone stood up and bowed before him in prostration. Utterly surprised, the warrior asked them what they were doing, but no one answered; they simply continued to bow. Finally a priest from among them gave him an explanation. The warrior said that the reason he had come to the medicinal spring was that he had been injured when he fell off his horse while hunting. However, everyone just continued to worship him. He remained perplexed for some time, and then the thought occurred to him, "I am actually Kannon; I must become a monk." He threw away his weapons and became a monk, and the people were deeply moved.

He went on to become a disciple of the famous priest Kakucho, and it was said that he lived in the province of Tosa thereafter.[1]

This story is noteworthy in that a man comes to find himself through someone else's dream. Before arriving at the hot spring he never doubts his identity as a warrior and is quite puzzled that others would regard him as Kannon simply on the basis of a voice in a dream. Yet, in the end he accepts this and becomes a monk. I like the fact that the story does not say the former warrior became a famous priest or saved many people. He is just an ordinary monk. That is enough to be a bodhisattva.

Most people would think such a warrior strange or weak because he determined his identity not by his own will or thought but through a stranger's dream, and I am sure that many Japanese would feel the same. However, this tendency is still at work on a subconscious level in the everyday life of the Japanese. Evidence for this can be seen in the use of the Japanese words for "I." There are many terms for the first person singular, such as *watakushi, boku, ore,* and *uchi.* The choice depends entirely on the circumstance and the person being addressed. In

1. *USM*, Ch. 6, No. 7 (89).

this respect it can be said that the Japanese finds "I" solely through the existence of others.

However, if this aspect is over-emphasized, one might conclude that the Japanese are so passive as to accept everything that comes their way and that they have no autonomy. The actual situation is more subtle. In order to help us understand personal autonomy in a Japanese context, let me refer to another dream episode from the *USM*:

> There was a man named Yoshio Tomo-no-Dainagon who was an attendant of the chief of Sado Province. He had a dream that he was standing with one foot on Todaiji and the other on Saidaiji [two major temples located in the east and west of the city of Nara, respectively]. When he told his wife about this dream, she interpreted it and said, "Your body will be torn in two." Yoshio was startled and thought that he had done something wrong.
>
> Later he went to see his lord who was skilled in reading faces. He invited Yoshio to enter and was unusually kind to him. Remembering what his wife had said, Yoshio became suspicious and thought that his lord was plotting to harm him. However, his lord told him that his face showed he had seen an auspicious dream; he had simply related it to the wrong person. As a consequence, he would get a high position in the course of his life but would be implicated in some crime. Sometime later Yoshio moved to Kyoto and received a high appointment but was accused of wrongdoing and lost his position. Everything turned out as his lord had said.[1]

This story shows the importance of the dreamer's attitude. Although Yoshio had an auspicious dream, his carelessness leads to misfortune. The next story illustrates the importance of keeping a dream secret:

1. *USM*, Ch. 1, No. 4 (4).

A certain man overheard a dream being told to a dream interpreter who told the dreamer that he would become a minister of state. Afterwards the first man asked the interpreter if he could buy the dream. The interpreter replied that he could, and instructed him to enter the room and relate the dream exactly as the dreamer had done. She gave him the same prediction, and he presented her with a gift. He eventually did become the minister of state while nothing special happened to the man who had actually had the dream.[1]

Like the previous episode, this story shows that having an auspicious dream is not enough. If one is careless it will lose its effect, but if one has a certain reverence, one can even buy dreams.

It is sometimes necessary to have the strength to hold on to them. Otherwise one may lose a blessing or even be subject to misfortune. A merely passive attitude towards dreams does not work.

5. The Concept of Nature

In considering the correlation between the human and the cosmic, we must ask ourselves what meaning Nature has for us. Jung says that the human being is an *opus contra naturam*. This paradoxical condition makes the issue very complicated, especially when we consider the situation in Japan where the concept of Nature is quite different from that of the West. Strictly speaking, the Japanese had no conception of Nature as such prior to their contact with Western culture.

As I have shown through the dream stories of medieval Japan, there was no distinct demarcation between life and death, reality and fantasy, myself and others. The

1. *USM*, Ch. 13, No. 5 (165).

same holds true for man and Nature. Throughout European history, Nature has been a concept which stands in opposition to culture and civilization, and continues to be objectified by human beings. The word "Nature" was translated into Japanese as *shizen,* 自然. Prior to this we did not have a concept of Nature. When we Japanese wish to talk about "Nature," we use such expressions as *sansen-somoku,* 山川草木 which literally means "the mountains, rivers, grasses, and trees." Akira Yanabu has pointed out the clear differences between the Japanese *shizen* and "Nature."[1] Many Japanese today confuse the two, causing a great deal of misunderstanding.

Let us see how the word *shizen,* 自然 was used before the encounter with the West. The term originated in China, and its oldest usage in literature is to be found in the Taoist writings of Lao Tzu (604? - 531 B.C.) and Chuang Tzu. It appears in the last line of the well-known twenty-fifth chapter of the *Tao Te Ching* which reads: *Tao Fa Tzu Jan,* 道法自然. Many attempts have been made to translate this, and here are just a few examples:

> "The way conforms to *its own nature.*" (Blackney)
> "Tao's standard is *the Spontaneous.* "(Fung Yu-lan)
> "The law of the Tao is *its own being.*" (James Legge)
> "Tao follows *its own ways.*" (Wu)
> "Tao is *by nature itself.* There is nothing which it could take for its model." (Ho Shang-Kung)

The difficulty of translating the term 自然 is readily apparent. The first important point is that it is not identical to "Nature." In fact it is not even a noun, and in premodern Japanese literature it was used almost exclusively as an adverb or adjective. It might be said that 自然 expresses a state in which everything flows spontaneously. There is something like an ever-changing flow in which

1. Akira Yanabu, *Honyaku no Shiso,* Heibon-sha, Tokyo, 1977.

everything – sky, earth, and man – is contained. Because it is like a continual process, it can never be grasped spatio-temporally, and strictly speaking, cannot be named. This state of 自然 was intuitively grasped by the Japanese and was originally read as *jinen* rather than the later *shizen*, which was used to translate "Nature."[1] The meaning of the two readings was identical until the Meiji Period (late 19th Century) when the latter was applied to the Western concept. *Shizen* never lost its original meaning, and the resulting failure to distinguish *jinen* from "Nature" has been the source of confusion. One point which these two terms do have in common is that both signify the opposite of artificiality. When the Japanese say that they like Nature, they are referring to a mixture of the two. One might say that *jinen* is more comprehensive than "Nature" and represents a standpoint embracing the latter. We may gain a better understanding of the stories I have related if we can sense what is meant by the former term. You and I, humans and Nature, reality and fantasy, flow spontaneously in *jinen*, which transcends all distinctions.

6. Ego, Self, and Nature

When the relation between human beings and the cosmos is examined psychologically, Jung's understanding

---

1. There are several Japanese adaptations of the Chinese readings for any given character. The two largest groupings are the *go on* and *kan on* readings. The former represent the Japanese approximations of the pronunciation of Chinese characters imported during the fifth and sixth centuries, while the latter represent approximations of the official Chinese pronunciations used in the capital of Chang-an during the 7th and 8th Centuries. ("On readings," *Kodansha* Encyclopedia of Japan, First Edition.) "*Jinen*" is the *go on* reading and "*shizen*" is the *kan on* reading.

of the relation between the ego and the Self becomes very important, and I would like to make use of his standpoint to help clarify the East Asian conception of the Self. I say "conception," but the Self can never actually be conceptualized.

Jung defined ego as the center of consciousness, and Self as the center of the psyche which encompasses both the realm of the conscious and the unconscious. He also stated that the Self cannot be known directly, but only through symbols and images which are accessible to consciousness. Thus, although the Self is the same for everyone, it appears differently to each person in accordance with the unique contents of his or her consciousness.

The Japanese words for ego, Self, and Nature are *jiga,* 自我, *jiko,* 自己, and *jinen,* 自然, respectively. It can be seen that they all have the character *ji,* 自 in common. Other readings for this character include *mizukara* and *onozukara*: paradoxically, they mean "voluntarily, of one's own free will," and "spontaneously, of itself." They may seem contradictory to the Westerner, but not to the Japanese. Perhaps it would be better to say that they are incommensurable from the standpoint of ego consciousness, but not from the standpoint of *jinen*. This two-fold sense of *ji* is contained in the Japanese understanding of ego, Self, and Nature.

Thus it may be said that dreams belong to the ego, the Self, and Nature, and that they all flow in *jinen* as originally understood by the Japanese.

We are led to the conclusion that everything in the cosmos flows as it is, and there is no need to speak of one thing symbolizing another. They are just there.

I have yet to clearly grasp the problem of Self and *jinen*, but I am inclined to say the following: The notion of the Self is basic to the hero myth, and in this context, human consciousness is inextricably bound to the ego. There may be another kind of consciousness in the reality of *jinen*; what Jung called the Self may be important, but in this context, it might be called by any number of names, or perhaps no name at all.

7. The Conscious, the Unconscious, and a Horse

Freud compared the relationship between the ego and the unconscious to that between a rider and his horse. With this in mind, let us examine the following dream seen by Myôe, a Buddhist priest of the thirteenth century:

> There was a big, clear pond. I climbed onto a large horse and played in the pond.
> The horse was unusually well fed. Then [I was] about to set out on a pilgrimage to Kumano.

Myôe goes on to comment:

> In [another] dream two or three nights previous, I playfully said, "How I would like to visit Kumano!" The priest Shinsho was there and reprimanded me: "You speak as if [you were] actually not [going]."
> I said to myself, "That is not so," and made a vow to go. [Thus] I reversed [my previous attitude], and now the dream is an auspicious sign [showing] that I truly wish to go. In addition, the large pond stands for meditation, and the horse for consciousness.[1]

---

1. Myôe Koben, *Myôe Shonin Yume no Ki* (MSYK), in *Myôe Shonin Shu*, compiled by Jun Kubota and Akio Yamaguchi, Iwanami Shoten, Tokyo, 1981, pp. 85-86 (389). I am indebted to Dr. George Joji Tanabe who has translated the entire *Dream Diary* as an appendix to his doctoral thesis on Myôe. I have made extensive use of his version in making my own translations. (George Joji Tanabe Jr., *Myôe Shonin (1173-1232): Tradition and Reform in Early Kamakura Buddhism*, Columbia University, Ph.D. Dissertation, 1983) The corresponding page numbers for Dr. Tanabe's translation appear in parentheses.

Freud might ask, "If the horse stands for consciousness, then what does Myôe the rider stand for?" Before
attempting to answer this question, I would like to relate
another dream which Myôe had about a year earlier
along with his commentary:

> I dreamt that I had constructed a pond which [covered an
> area of] about a half to three quarters of an acre. There was
> hardly any water in it. A sudden downpour filled the pond
> with pure, clear water. There was another large pond next to
> it that seemed to be an old river. When the small one was
> full, there was [only] about one foot separating it from the
> larger one. If it rained just a little more, [the small pond]
> would merge with the larger pond. I felt that if they merged,
> the fish, turtles, and other [creatures] could move over to
> the small pond. It seemed to be the fifteenth day of the
> second month. I thought, "Tonight the moon will rise over
> this pond and is sure to be splendid."
>
> Interpretation: The small pond is meditation. The large
> pond is the fundamental *samadhi* to which all the Buddhas
> and bodhisattvas have awakened. The fish and other [crea-
> tures] are all sages. Each being was deeply significant, and I
> contemplated this [fact]. The lack of water stands for the
> time of no practice. Now, even with a little faith, all the
> Buddhas and bodhisattvas can come through. The absence
> of fish in the small pond at the beginning [represents] the
> initial aspiration [for enlightenment].[1]

I have little to add to Myôe's own interpretation. Please
note that in the lunar calendar, the moon is full on the
fifteenth day of the month.

The splendid full moon represents the fullness of deep
meditation, but the fact that Myôe is absent indicates that
he saw the truth but did not experience it. He is waiting
for the fundamental *samadhi* of the large pond to flow
into the small one. Returning to the first dream I men-

1. *MSYK,* p. 77 (89).

tioned (which took place about one year later), we find Myôe riding on a horse and about to set out on a pilgrimage to Kumano, one of the major centers of religious worship in Japan. One might say that he made the transition from observer to actor, except that Myôe tells us the horse stands for consciousness, not himself. Then what does Myôe stand for? My answer is that he is *jinen*, the spontaneous flow of being. My translation reads, "Then [I was] about to set out on a pilgrimage to Kumano," but the subject is omitted in the original as is often the case in Japanese. It might be interesting to think that the subject is neither the horse nor Myôe, but *jinen*, which includes both.

8. A Constitution Based on Jinen

Myôe lived during one of the most important periods of Japanese political history. In the Jokyu Disturbance of 1221, an attempt by the retired Emperor Go-Toba's imperial faction to wrest control from the military government failed. This led to an increase in the political power of the government in Kamakura, and Yasutoki Hojo became the military regent in the imperial capital of Kyoto. Myôe greatly influenced Yasutoki, who made many revolutionary changes based on the former's world-view. This does not mean that Yasutoki made Buddhism or Myôe's Huayen the state religion. On the contrary there is virtually no external evidence of Myôe's contribution, which was actually more far-reaching than the establishment of religious institutions.

Until Yasutoki became the regent, the Japanese constitution had been basically an imitation of the Chinese. Yasutoki felt the necessity for a new order, but it was neither possible nor desirable to abolish the old system. He

skillfully put his ideals into effect by establishing a catalogue of practical law which did not replace the constitution, at least not in appearance. He stressed the fact that
the old law did not fulfill the needs of the present age,
and said the new catalogue consisted of what he simply
felt was reasonable, that it was not based on anything in
particular. To effect such a comprehensive transformation of the national constitution and say that it was based
on nothing is remarkable. The power of the new catalogue can be understood as a reflection of *jinen*.

Yasutoki once asked Myôe how to rule the nation, and
the latter replied that a statesman should be like a good
doctor who cures an illness by rooting out its real cause.
The cause of disturbance in Japan was greed, and if Yasutoki wished to remedy this, he had to abolish his own.
Yasutoki expressed doubt that others would remain
greedy even if he were able to get rid of his own desire.
Myôe answered that if Yasutoki really became free of his
own, the entire nation would naturally follow. It is the
idea that the state one attains is the state of the world.
Yasutoki actually made efforts to put Myôe's advice into
practice and has been praised as a noble statesman ever
since.

Myôe did not say how the nation would be freed of
desire if Yasutoki eliminated his. The former explained
neither the relationship between an individual and his
world, nor the nature of one person's influence on another. In order to understand the basis of Myôe's advice,
we must examine the teaching of the Hua-yen.

9. *Yüan-ch'i in the Hua-yen School*

Although Myôe was relatively open to the various Buddhist schools and teachings which had found their way to

Japan, he was primarily a student of the Hua-yen School. In the *Hua-yen Ching,* or *The Sutra of the Flower Garland,* all things freely interpenetrate each other. This complete mutual penetration and permeation is beautifully captured in a phrase which appears often: "Even a speck of dust contains all the Buddhas."

In 1980, Toshihiko Izutsu gave a talk on the philosophy of the Hua-yen. I would like to quote a passage from his presentation in order to illuminate just one aspect of Hua-yen thought, the notion of *yüan-ch'i* (Jap. *Engi*) as elaborated by the Chinese Hua-yen master, Fa-Ts'ang (643-712):

> ... nothing in this world exists independently of others. Everything depends for its phenomenal existence upon everything else. All things are correlated with one another. All things mutually originate ... Thus the universe in this vista is a tightly structured nexus of multifariously and manifoldly interrelated ontological events, so that even the slightest change in the tiniest part cannot but effect all the other parts.[1]

The quintessence of the Hua-yen *yüan-ch'i* is "the dynamic, simultaneous, and interdependent emergence and existence of all things." It is important to note here that *yüan-ch'i* is not based on linear causality. Izutsu uses the following diagram to illustrate the Huayen cosmology.

In this diagram each letter stands for some phenomenon or entity. From the standpoint of "X," all other phenomena ("A," "B," "C,"...) are the formative factors of "X." The situation is the same from the standpoint of any other phenomenon, such as "K," "A," "B," "C," and so on, ad infinitum. I feel that this diagram aptly describes the

---

1. Toshihiko Izutsu, "The Nexus of Ontological Events: A Buddhist View of Reality" in *Eranos 49-1980,* pp. 384-85.

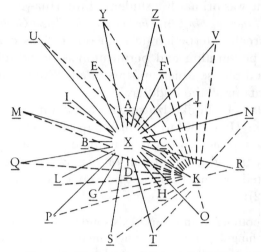

Figure 2. Illustration of yüan-ch'i *thinking*

Kannon story. The warrior comes to the realization that he is Kannon through the formative influence of the people around him, who correspond to the letters in this diagram. It is said in the *Hua-yen Ching*:

> If one begins to seek to become a bodhisattva, one will understand that a small world is a large world, and a large world, a small world. Moreover, a small world is many worlds, and many worlds, a small world. A wide world is a narrow world. A world is limitless. A defiled world is a pure world, and a pure world, a defiled world.[1]

Thus, one is all, and all is one. Because Myôe had awakened to this truth himself, he was able to advise Yasutoki that if he behaved correctly, the whole nation would follow.

If one is all, the problem of individual identity presents

1. *Hua-yen Ching.* The *Hua-yen Ching* has been translated into English by Thomas Cleary, *The Flower Ornament Scripture: The Avatamsaka Sutra,* Volume I, Shambhala, Boston, 1984; *The Flower Ornament Scripture: The Avatamsaka Sutra,* Volume II, Shambhala, Boston, 1986.

itself: How can "A" be distinguished from "B"? Izutsu explained this in terms of Fa-Ts'ang's notion of ontological "powerfulness" and "powerlessness." Each phenomenon ("A," "B," "C,"...) possesses identical contents, but takes on various appearances according to the amount of power being exerted by any given element:

> Those elements that happen to be "powerless" in a thing are not manifest, only the "powerful" and dominant elements being empirically actualized. Nevertheless they are there, all of them as part of the depth-structure of the thing, supposing, as it were, from below the phenomenal subsistence of the thing as that very thing.[1]

From the standpoint of depth psychology, I would like to say that the meaning of "powerless" and "powerful" becomes relative, and depends upon the condition of consciousness. To ordinary consciousness, only the manifestations of "powerful" elements are visible, but perhaps in other realms (such as the dream state), "powerless" components can be seen as well. One's father appears as a catfish, or one can stand with one foot on Todaiji Temple and the other on Saidaiji.

I would like to relate another dream that Myôe had:

> I thought I was going somewhere. Then I arrived at the gate of the Great Minister of Ichijo, where there was a single black dog. It rubbed itself against my feet and became very friendly. I had thought in my mind that I had raised this dog in years past. I did not see it when I went out today; I arrived at this gate and was waiting for it. I had wondered when it would come here; now we are together and we should not part. That dog was like a pony; it was a young dog with fur of dazzling color. It seemed as if it had been brushed with a comb.[2]

1. Izutsu, *ibid.*, p. 391.
2. *MSYK*, p. 90 (131).

Perhaps the friendly black dog which he thought he had raised is a "powerless" component in him which he had not been conscious of. It is a sign of Myôe's wisdom that once he had become aware of its existence, he decides they should not part. It is important to accept the existence of "powerless" elements in oneself, whether they take the form of a black dog or something else. Here is another dream from about the same time:

> [During my early evening meditation, when I wished to perform esoteric practices], there was a very dignified, beautiful lady in a room. Her clothing was exquisite, but she showed no sign of worldly desire. I was in the same place, but I did not feel any affection for her and ignored her. She was quite fond of me and did not wish to be separated. I [continued to] ignore her and left. She still showed no sign of worldly desire. The lady held a mirror around which she wrapped some wire. She also held a large sword.
>
> Interpretation: The woman was [the Buddha] Vairocana: she was certainly the queen.[1]

Myôe strictly adhered to the monastic code, and unlike most priests of his time, obeyed the precept which forbids touching of women. His attitudes are reflected in this dream, since he rejects the woman who does not want to be separated from him and leaves her. In the interpretation, however, he tells us that she is the Tathagata Vairocana, the Sun Buddha, who is the central figure of the *Hua-yen Ching*. Although Vairocana is cosmic and transcendental, he is usually depicted in male form. The fact that Myôe calls Vairocana "the queen" indicates that he sees the female aspect of the deity.

According to the Hua-yen view of *yüan-ch'i* Vairocana is manifest in all phenomena, but Myôe's choice to observe the precept on women entails a rejection of an aspect of

1. *MSYK*, p. 89 (12).

the deity. I believe this is what Myôe meant by his interpretation. A priest is supposed to maintain the monastic code, but doing so paradoxically implies the exclusion of a part of one's eternal reality. There is no way to have both. One must make an exclusive choice with full commitment and be aware of the dark side which necessarily accompanies it.

10. Turning Point

What is the role of the human being in the reality of *jinen* if everything including the former is simply flowing spontaneously of itself? In other words, what is the role of the ego? In the East the importance of diminishing the power of the ego has been emphasized in order to make one's life conform to *jinen,* but I do not feel that this provides a satisfactory answer. In order to probe this question more deeply, let us turn to another episode from the *USM* which has evolved into the well-known folk tale, "The Straw Millionaire":

> A young warrior who was completely alone in this world arrived at the temple of Hasedera where a statue of Kannon was enshrined. He prayed to Kannon and vowed not to leave until he received a message in a dream. Afraid that he would starve and cause a disturbance, the monks of the temple offered him some food. Twenty-one days later, he had a dream in which a man emerged from the altar where Kannon was enshrined and told the warrior to leave and keep everything which came into his possession.
>
> Just as he went through the temple gate, he fell down and clutched a single stalk of straw. Remembering the dream, he got up and walked on with the straw in his hand. Shortly thereafter a fly began to pester him, so he tied it to the end

of his straw. Further down the road a woman of the nobility, her son, and their retinue were approaching on their way to worship at Hasedera. The son said that he wished to have the fly and straw, and the warrior told one of the retainers: "Although these are gifts from the Buddha, I will give them to him." The mother was grateful for his generosity and gave him three oranges. He thought, "A single stalk of straw has been transformed into three oranges."

Another woman of the nobility approached with her retinue; one of her servants told the warrior that she was tired and thirsty but that they could not find any water for her. The warrior offered her the oranges, and she gave him three rolls of cloth as an expression of her gratitude. He thought, "The stalk of straw has become three rolls of cloth."

The next day he saw a man riding on a magnificent horse but the latter suddenly died before his eyes. Thinking that this was a sign the horse was meant to be his, he bought the horse with a roll of cloth. He then turned towards the Kannon enshrined at Hasedera and prayed, "Please bring this horse back to life." The horse opened its eyes and stood up, and he was overjoyed. He exchanged the other two rolls of cloth for a saddle and other gear and set off for Kyoto. There he exchanged the horse for a house and rice fields, and he eventually became a wealthy man.[1]

The young warrior is quite passive, just accepting what comes his way. However, his attitude changes when he sees the horse die. He actively seeks to purchase the horse and prays to Kannon to resurrect it. It is a great gamble on his part, for no one expects the horse to revive. This act of full commitment is the turning point of the story. Similar scenes can be found in many Japanese stories, and constitute the most important point in the development of the protagonist.

Without the turning point, the hero would have been destroyed by his own passivity. But such points cannot be

1. *USM*, Ch. 7, No. 5 (96).

realized without full commitment, which is in turn accompanied by danger. If the horse had not revived, the hero would have been lost.

How and when does a person know that his turning point has come? What are the criteria for determining it? The answer is obvious: Follow *jinen*. I know this is meaningless from the so-called scientific point of view, but perhaps my point can be made more apparent by examining the notion of individuality.

When one's individuality is established by means of making clear distinctions between oneself, others, things, and Nature, many general laws for observing the world can be discovered. By applying these laws Nature can be efficiently controlled. However, one cannot establish one's uniqueness as long as one is under the rule of the collective consciousness; a catfish remains a catfish and a warrior cannot become Kannon. The objective path to individuality does not allow one's father to become a catfish or a warrior to become a bodhisattva.

On the other hand, one may lead a unique life if one is open to others. Yet, this path is open to danger; one may believe that a catfish can be one's father, but also lose one's life. In Jungian terms, one's individuality may be lost in the collective unconscious.

A truly individual life requires unique turning points as well as general rules. Although by definition there are no rules for these turning points, we can increase our sensitivity to them through reading stories with full commitment. Our dreams are actually these stories, bestowed upon each of us in the realm beyond distinctions, in *jinen*.

Figure 3. Image and Verse on the Nine Aspects

II. Bodies in the Dream Diary of Myôe

1. Myôe

Myôe is a Japanese Buddhist priest who was born in 1173 and died in 1232. He belonged to the Hua-yen (Keg-on in Japanese) sect. During Myôe's lifetime several new Buddhist sects arose simultaneously. Myôe's sect was a traditional one and he fought against these new religious movements. He is still revered by many in Japan. One reason is that he is one of the few priests who faithfully kept the precept not to have intimate relationships with women.

Myôe is also an extraordinary person who keeps a dream diary from his 19th until his 58th year, the year before his death. Half of his diary is still extant so we can actually "read" his dreams. Sometimes he writes down his interpretations as well. There are many literatures of the world in which single dreams are mentioned, but as far as I know Myôe may be the first person in the world to keep a full dream diary.

Myôe's father was a warrior and his mother the daughter of a warrior. It is said in a biography of Myôe that his parents both had dreams before he was born. His father went to a temple and prayed for a boy. Then he had a dream. Somebody came out from the inside of the temple and said to him, "Your wish will be fulfilled." That person then pierced his right ear with a stick. His mother also prayed for a son. When she slept with her younger sister, she dreamed she received oranges from some-body's hand. That same night, her sister also had a dream in which two oranges were given to her. But the older sister, Myôe's mother, was watching and said that the oranges were intended for her. The older sister thereupon took the oranges from the younger sister's hands. Sometime later, the older one conceived and gave birth to Myôe. After he had become a priest, Myôe interprets the dream to mean that the two oranges represent the two sects of Buddhism, Hua-yen and Chen-yen (Kegon and Shingon in Japanese). Although Myôe belongs to the Hua-yen sect, he studies Chen-yen and combines the two in practice.

When Myôe is four years old, his father puts a warrior's hat on the boy's head and says jokingly, "Nice looking boy! You can be the follower of a court noble." Myôe is greatly disturbed to hear this as he already desires to be a priest. He thus tries to damage his good looks, by attempting to fall down from the corridor which opens onto the garden. But that attempt is frustrated by someone who grabs him from behind. He next tries to burn his face with a glowing iron, but terrified by the heat of the burning iron, he fails. Hence from the very beginning of his life Myôe has the tendency to negate his body.

Myôe's parents die when he is nine years old – the one following the other. After their deaths, he leaves his home and enters a temple. At 16, he becomes a priest and concentrates fully on his vocation: *sîla* (precepts), *samâdhi* (meditation) and *prajnâ* (wisdom). At that time, Japanese priests in general do not keep the precepts. Many of them, instead of gaining wisdom through meditation, try to accumulate knowledge in order to become high-ranking priests. Myôe cannot stand this trend and bitterly denounces it. He retires to a mountain and lives alone to avoid secularized Buddhism. There, at 19, he begins to keep a dream diary. Even though his desire to stay in the countryside is very strong, he yields to the father of the emperor, Gotôba, who asks him to become the master of Kozanji Temple at the age of 34.

In both meditations and dreams Myôe sees many religious figures and symbols, and has many telepathic experiences. He becomes one of the most famous priests in Japan defending traditional Buddhism against the newly rising sects. Then at 60, he dies calmly in accord with the Buddhist formula for dying, surrounded by many of his disciples. His last words are, "I come from where precepts are fulfilled."

One of his acquaintances comes to know of Myôe's death in the following dream: Myôe is climbing up the Buddhist tower which reaches to the clouds; many of his disciples and others gather around the tower. Another acquaintance dreams that Myôe is standing in a purple cloud which comes from the West. (West is supposed to be the direction of Nirvana.) Similar dreams are reported by several others.

2. The First Dream

Although he keeps a dream diary from his 19th year, Myôe has other dreams that are mentioned in two early biographies. One is recorded by his disciple Kikai. The other, while often attributed to Kikai, is of uncertain origin. I will use both as references since they reflect an image of Myôe which the Japanese hold.

The first dream comes at 9 years of age when Myôe enters the temple. In the dream his late nurse is dismembered with the parts of her body scattered around. She suffered extraordinary pain. Although he knows she had been a sinful woman, he feels especially sad. He thinks he must become a good priest in order to rescue her in life after death.

Compare Myôe's first recorded dream with that of the 4 year old C.G. Jung.[1] In that dream, Jung sees something which looks like a tree trunk, "made of skin and naked flesh, and on top there was something like a rounded head with no face and no hair." Both dreams are about the body. Yet their content is completely different. What Jung sees is a big phallus under the ground, whereas Myôe sees a dismembered female body. Though different, both dreams have a tremendous numinosity which both men have to confront for the rest of their lives.

Let us consider the dismembered female body in Myôe's first dream in relation to the Buddhist ideas about the female and about the body. When Gautama establishes Buddhism, he thinks only of men becoming priests and gaining enlightenment through meditation. He fails to consider women. His is a paternally oriented religion. Soon afterwards, the strong maternal psychology prevailing in India merges with it, and Buddhist teaching gradually changes.

When Buddhism is imported into Japan, the maternal aspect is already strong. The Japanese import Buddhism without its precepts. The precept of not touching a woman, for example, is not kept by the Japanese priests. Gotôba, the father of the emperor of Myôe's era, once said, "One who really does not is Buddha; one who does *secretly* is a priest." While Japanese appreciate the maternal principle, that in itself does not mean that they appreciate women. For example, when Myôe's mother prays for a son, she says, "I got the chance to be a human being, but a woman cannot again be reborn a human in the next life as she is so stupid. I pray, please give me a son who can

1. *Memories, Dreams, Reflections* by *C.G. Jung,* recorded and edited by Aniela Jaffé, translated by Richard and Clara Winston; New York and London, 1963, pp. 11-12.

rescue me in my life after death." In reincarnation, women are not supposed to be born again as human beings.

The combination of this prevailing maternal principle and the underestimation of women allows Japanese men to easily have sexual relations with women. They do not give sex a special value but take it for granted. In this case, the sexual relation does not have the symbolic meaning of the union of opposites, but simply going back into the maternal uroboros. After establishing the paternal principle, the sexual relations come to have an ambivalent meaning. First it means evil. Thus priests are forbidden to touch women. It can, however, have the symbolic meaning of union.

Myôe's dream reflects the fact that the women of the time were in great distress as human beings. It is a situation of complete disintegration. His task is to rescue her from that situation. In order to see how he does it, we must first understand his way of relating to women and to the body.

3. Discarding the Body

Compared with other priests of his day, Myôe has a unique attitude toward women. He keeps the precepts strictly. He has a negative attitude toward his body. He already tried to injure his body when he was only four. Another indication of this tendency comes in his thirteenth year. He says, "I have become old enough as I am thirteen years old." Whereupon he tries to throw away his body. At that time, ordinary people are not placed in cemeteries after death. They are simply laid down in a designated place. At night, dogs and wolves come and devour them. Myôe goes to that kind of place and lays his body down to await darkness. Wolves eventually appear, but eat only dead bodies, and not Myôe.

Throwing away the body is an important act in Buddhism. Some stories about it are in related Buddhist scriptures. One Bodhisattva, for example, throws his body away in order to feed a hungry tiger. The idea is that one sacrifices his body for others. This is the most precious sacrifice one can offer Buddha. One of the reasons for Myôe's brave but naïve intention might stem from his warrior heritage. When he fails to carry out his self sacrifice, he realizes that he cannot die if fate does not decree it even though he himself has decided on it. It is quite understandable that he says that he has become old enough when he was only 13. I have the feeling that every child reaches a kind of completeness without adult sexuality. He is a puer and a senex at the same time. A person like Myôe can recognize his senex side at that age and say: I am old enough. I imagine Myôe feels this kind of completeness, and has the notion that this completeness would be destroyed if he kept his life. The destructive power of sexuality is obviously at hand.

In connection with the throwing away of the body, I would like to mention a picture story called, "The Pictures of the Nine Phases." In ancient Japan, there were many scrolls of picture stories. One shows how outer reality is vain or empty. The first picture shows the dead body of a noble lady. The following pictures realistically show the successive process of decay until the corpse is eaten by dogs and nothing is left. Each picture is accompanied by a poem which precisely describes the features of the changing of the dead body. This scroll is used for priests' contemplation upon the transitoriness of outer reality.

The first time I saw the pictures, I was shocked not only by the realistic portrayal of the decay of the human body, but also by the fact that the dying figure was not a male, but a female. The person who is contemplating these images is a man, the priest. He is contemplating not himself but his anima. I came to the terrible intuitive conclusion that the anima must have died in Japanese culture in this era, or that Japanese culture has been established at the cost of the anima.

I thought about this over again and again because I did not wish to accept this conclusion. Yet I cannot deny it.

My current thought on the matter is that the anima is an archetype. Its images do not have to be represented by women figures. The anima function works in Japanese culture through various images. One may say, however, that those parts of the anima represented by a young female figure as an individual did die in Japanese culture. Who can save her? This has been a great recurring problem for the Japanese.

Returning to Myôe's dreams, I would like to present a short but very important dream which he had between his 16th and 19th years. In the dream, Myôe goes into a room in a temple where he sees the famous priest, Kûkai, sleeping. Kûkai's two eyes looked like crystals, and they are lying beside a pillow. Kûkai gives them to Myôe who places them in a sleeve of his robe. (One can easily keep things in the long sleeves of a kimono.)

Kûkai is one of the most prominent priests in the history of Japan. He was born in 774 and died in 835. He went to China and brought Chen-yen (shingon) back to Japan. Myôe belonged to the Hua-yen sect but at the same time studied Shingon. Kûkai is in this sense a predecessor of Myôe. The two crystal eyes which Myôe receives remind us of the two oranges in his mother's dream, a theme to which I shall return later. Here I need only point out that Myôe inherited, so to say, the eyes of his prominent predecessor, the tools by which one can see the world.

4. The Mother of Buddhas

Soon after he fails to accomplish his self-sacrifice, Myôe has a dream in which his body is eaten by wolves. Later, when he relates this dream to his disciples, he notes that this is the kind of dream in which one dreams what he wants to do in his awakened state. It is an extraordinary thing to experience one's own death in dreams, as Myôe did. One has a dream of one's own death when a rapid change is going to occur. Myôe's dream surely denotes that, yet it also shows the possibility of the transformation of the body.

From his 19th year, Myôe takes Butsugen-Butsumo (one of the esoteric Buddhist deities) as his personal deity and concentrates on praying to this being. The literal meaning of Butsugen-Butsumo is Buddha's eyes. She is supposed to be the Mother of all Buddhas. According to the dreams in his biographies, Myôe feels maternal mercy in Butsugen.

Around his 20th year, he has a series of dreams. In one he is in a run-down old house. There he is terrified by many snakes and scorpions. Butsugen appears and takes him in her arms so that he can escape from that horrible place. In another, when Myôe goes along a dangerous mountain path on horseback. Butsugen helps him, leading the horse. Finally he has a dream in which he identifies himself with Butsugen. Some heavenly children carry him on a beautiful palanquin and call out, "Butsugen! Butsugen!" He thinks he has already become Butsugen.

It is worthwhile noting that Myôe's identification with the Great Mother occurred after he had experienced a strong negation of his body, namely, his attempt at self-sacrifice and the dream of being eaten by wolves. This is not a regression into the maternal Uroboros in a bodily dimension. Since his mother had died when he was still a child, it is quite understandable that he was impressed with the maternal aspect of Buddha. When we think of the dichotomy of the paternal principle and the maternal principle, spirit and body, we tend to equate the paternal with spirit and the maternal with body. But we must not forget that thinking in dichotomy already relies on the paternal principle. Hence the identification with the Mother does not necessarily mean a one-sided bodily experience. It has, rather, both bodily and spiritual aspects. I am sure that, after experiencing the Mother's acceptance, Myôe's suicidal intention vanished.

5. Cutting off the Ear and the Appearance of Mañjusri Boddhisattva

Myôe continues his study of Buddhist scriptures and meditation. In due course, his aversion towards secularized Buddhism becomes stronger and stronger until, at 23, he decides to retreat to a mountain where he is alone. In his life of seclusion he eats little food, none of which is cooked.

Myôe's hatred of secularized Buddhism increases. It reaches a highpoint when he decides to cut off his ear. He bitterly accuses other priests of being proud of their beautiful robes or high social positions. In order to show how he has no interest in the secular life, he decides to injure his body. Tonsure is not enough for him. If he cuts off his nose, the remaining mucus would stain the holy scriptures. If he puts out his eyes, he would be unable to read the scriptures. If he cuts his hands off, he would not be able to form the mudras. He can, however, cut off his ear, because it would still be possible to hear sermons. Thus he cuts off his right ear in front of Butsugen-Butsumo, the Mother of Buddhas. In a dream, that same night, an Indian priest appears and says that he has been recording priests' sacrifices and that Myôe's deed has been recorded. Myôe awakes after he sees several big notebooks for recording sacrifices. The dream shows that his deed is not an impulsive self injury but is acknowledged and recorded by his psyche as a noble sacrifice.

Cutting off his ear obviously follows the pattern expressed in a desire to throw away his body. Although he has given up his intention of suicide, he must have been thinking all along how he could sacrifice his body to the Buddha. Cutting off an ear in Myôe's case denotes self-castration, which none but creative persons can do.

Soon after he cuts his ear off, he is pleased to see Mañjusri Bodhisattva appear to him in a dream. It is the first dream in his diary. His biographers tell us how impressed he is by this dream, although the description in his dream diary is rather short, and does not indicate any of this feeling. His dream diary simply says, "25th of the same month. I did contemplation upon Nothingness in front of the Buddha. Mañjusri Bodhisattva appeared in the air. He was golden and sat on a lion. He was about one meter tall."

Mañjusri is known as a Boddhisattva of wisdom. After Myôe experiences the identification with the Great Mother, the male figure of wisdom appears. We can now recognize that Myôe's psychology is not only based on the maternal principle but is also beginning to include the paternal one. No wonder he has the following dream soon after the dream of Mañjusri: Two beautiful peacocks bring two scrolls to him. The one has a title of Butsugen and the other Shakya. Myôe is so impressed that he weeps, praying to Butsugen and Shakya. In this dream the theme of the number two appears again. This time, however, the number two denotes the combination of the paternal and maternal aspects of the Buddha.

6. Ascending

It is natural that Myôe has dreams which have something to do with the theme of ascending after communicating with the paternal side of the Buddha. In one dream, he sees many rocks making a straight line in the sea. They are fifty-two rocks which denote the fifty-two stages leading to Boddhisattva. He jumps onto the first stone, where there are many priests and ordinary people. He goes to the second, but no one follows him. He goes on and on, and finally reaches the last one. He can see the universe from that point. Then he goes back to the first one and tells the people about his experience. In another dream, he tries to climb up a tower. When he gets to the top and wants to reach a star, he awakes. About two weeks later he has the same kind of dream and the story continues. This time, he succeeds in reaching the star. From there he can see the whole universe. In those two dreams Myôe reaches the remotest places. The second dream reminds me of the visions which Jung has during his severe illness:[1] While having these dreams in his remote retreat, Myôe is in bad physical condition because he has eaten so little. The dreams of both Jung and Myôe show a state where their imaginal bodies are in lofty positions, when their material bodies are very near collapse.

Although Myôe has deep religious experiences through dreams and visions during his life of seclusion, he becomes severely ill. He suffers from acute diarrhoea. One day he is miraculously cured by dreaming and drinks a sort of warm soup given by an Indian priest. It seems that the Buddha acknowledges Myôe's sacrifice of the body and rewards him for it.

1. *Memories, Dreams, Reflections*, pp. 289-98.

7. Longing for the Buddha

When he is about 30, Myôe has a strong wish to go to India. His main concern is with the Buddha as a real person. He tells his followers that he would not have done any meditation or studies of scriptures if he could have been born in the Buddha's era. He would have been content just to live with the living Buddha. His longing for the Buddha is so great that he finally decides to visit India with some of his disciples. However, he is forced to abandon his intention because of some miraculous happenings.

At 31, one of his relatives, a lady, becomes possessed by Kasuga-Myojin, one of the Shinto deities. She tells him not to go to India. Myôe believes in Kasuga-Myojin. Though it seems strange to us today, at that time in Japan people believed that Japanese Shinto deities were also manifestations of the Buddha. Belief in Kasuga-Myojin thus presents no problem for Myôe. When the lady is possessed, she goes up on the top of a door and tells Myôe and his disciples that they should stay in Japan and be a guide for Japanese people. While she is talking, the whole room is filled with fragrance. After her talk she embraces and caresses Myôe. He is deeply moved and bursts into tears. Yielding to the oracle of Kasuga Myôe discards his intention to visit India. Coincidentally, it is the same year that Buddhism in India was destroyed by the invading Moslems.

Even though Myôe gives up his trip, his wish to go to the Buddha's land arises again, two years later. This time, he calculates the distance to India and figures out when the country could be reached. The record of his calculation is still kept in the Kozanji Temple. When he decides to go to India this time he suffers from a strange illness. Myôe senses somebody is beside him. When he is about to tell of his proposed journey that person pinches Myôe's belly, inflicting a strong pain. When he continues to talk with his followers about his intention to visit India that person gets on Myôe's belly and presses his breasts with his hands. Myôe is nearly tormented to death. He wonders whether this is also a message from Kasuga, but he is not quite sure so he draws lots of "should go" or "should not go" three times, and each time receives negative results. On one of these occasions, when in front of Shakya, one lot falls down from the table. He makes a great effort to find it, but in vain. He thereupon retrieves the one left on the table only to find the result is "should not go." Before this event, he had a dream. He saw two flying white herons. Suddenly a person in white clothes shot an arrow, killing one of the birds which fell down. After the event, he realized that the dream is an omen reflecting the losing of the lot.

Myôe gives up his intention to go to India. His abandonment here recalls his abandonment of his intention to throw off his body. Even though his longing for the Buddha's land is very strong, he has to abandon it. Through these experiences, Myôe begins to realize that he does not have to go to Buddha's land since the land in which he is living can be the Buddha land as well.

8. Matter and Psyche

Myôe belongs to the Hua-Yen (Kegon) sect.
A teaching of Hua-yen says:

> The Buddha is likened to the Psyche.
> The people are likened to the Buddha.
> Between the Buddha, the People, and the Psyche
> There is no distinction.

Myôe's whole life, one might argue, is a realization of
this Hua-Yen teaching. For Myôe, one's life as a whole is
much more important than what he says or what he
thinks. Myôe experiences many synchronistic events. One
day when he is meditating Myôe calls for one of his followers and asks him to rescue a bee which has fallen into
a basin. The follower is surprised at hearing this but he
goes to the basin only to find that what Myôe said was
true. Many of these kinds of events are reported in the
biographies. In the dream diary, Myôe records telepathic
dreams as well.

Yasunari Kawabata, the Nobel prize-winning Japanese
novelist, speaks about Myôe's poems in the Nobel ceremony. In his talk, "Japan, the Beautiful, and Myself,"
Kawabata recites a few of Myôe's poetic lines:

> Winter moon, coming from the clouds to keep me
>   company,
> Is the wind piercing, the snow cold?

And again:

> I shall go behind the mountain
> Go there, too, O moon –
> Night after night we shall keep each other company.

In Myôe's explanations of these poems, he feels that
the moon is keeping him secret company. While he sits in
Zen meditation on a cold night, the moon is his companion.

Myôe sees psyche in matter. He wants to write a letter
to a cherry tree he loves, but he does not dare to do so
because he is afraid that people would think he had gone
mad. He loves his beautiful island called Karuma. Eventually he no longer cares what others might think about
him. When combined with his sense of humor, he goes so
far as to write a letter to his beloved island. One of his

disciples takes the letter quite seriously and wonders how he can deliver it. Myôe answers him that he should go to the island and shout loudly, "This is the letter from Myôe!" and just leave it anywhere on the island.

Although he experiences many synchronistic events, Myôe never loses his ability to test the reality of the outer world. When some of his followers are so deeply impressed with Myôe's telepathic ability that they believe that he is a reincarnation of Buddha, Myôe is very sad. He says that those things are not miracles at all, that any person who meditates and follows the Buddha's teachings might easily have the same experiences. They happen naturally. He was never proud of his telepathic experiences.

At about 40, Myôe had the following interesting dream:

I got a stone. It was 3 cm high, 2.1 cm wide and 0.6 cm thick. There was an eye in the stone, about 1.5 cm long and 0.6-0.9 cm wide. The color of the eye was white, not pure white, but a bit darkened. Because of this eye, the stone had a spiritual power. It moved, jumping like a living creature. I held it with my right hand and showed it to my master. When I put it down, it moved like a fish on the land. My master was very much pleased to see it. I said that the name of the stone was *sekigan*. (The word means Stone-eye.) A kind of fish was hung on the roof at that moment. The inside of the fish decayed and became nothing. One of the fish's eyes looked like that it was about to come out and moved a bit. I told this to my master. Beside it there was a kind of dried animal. It was dried but the skin was not dried and remained just like an ordinary one. I wanted to take and to show the fish to my master. A woman came in there and took it. The animal had four legs. There were holes on its back. The woman said 'How should it be possible that I, such a noble being, killed this kind of animal?' I thought, the animal was a noble lady. I felt pity for this creature and consoled it.

When it was laid down on the earth, the animal said, 'Please hang me again just like before.' I thought that it was so accustomed to being hanged that it wanted to be so again. It seemed that the creature felt extraordinary pain. One of his arms was cut. I hung it again as it wanted. The master was the Buddha. The woman was Mañjusri Bodhisattva. The noble lady was the Mother of Buddhas. The eye of the stone (Sekigan) should be stronger than that of the animal.

In the dream the stone not only has an eye but also moves like an animal. The fact that Myôe takes these persons who appear in the dream as the Buddha, Bodhisattva, and the Mother of Buddhas, shows how important he feels this dream to be. I imagine he is struck by the fact that a stone becomes alive in the dream.

With his enlightenment in the Hua-Yen teaching about matter and psyche, Myôe reaches the extreme point where he does not care about salvation in the next life. The most important thing for him is "just to be as it should be."

9. The Dream of Zenmyô

After the abandonment of his intention to go to India Myôe begins to have dreams of female figures. He dreams that he climbs a rocky mountain with a young lady. He climbs with her hand in hand. After that, female figures appear in his dreams from time to time. In general, Myôe has good relationships with the women in his dreams. Female figures reach their highest point in a dream which he has when he is 48 years old.

Juzôbô (one of his disciples) brought me a kind of pottery for incense. I thought somebody had brought it from China to him. Its inside was divided into several parts which contained about twenty various Chinese figurines. Among them there were figures of two tortoises mating. There was a Chinese woman figure about fifteen cm in size. This was also a piece of china-ware. Somebody said that the woman figure felt sad as she was sent to Japan from China. I asked her, 'Do you feel sad to come here?' She nodded. I said, 'I would like to caress you. Don't be so sad!' She denied it. I took her from the container. She was weeping. One could see the tears in her eyes. Her tears flowed down and wet her shoulders. She was so sad to come to Japan. She found her voice and said, 'It is of no use to do so.' I answered, 'If I am only a priest, it would be so. However, in this country, everybody worships me as a saint. As such a person, I would like to caress you.' The woman figure seemed to be very pleased to hear this and said, 'Then, would you caress me?' I accepted. Suddenly the figure turned into a real woman. I thought that tomorrow there would be some Buddhist ceremony and would like to bring her with me. She wanted to go with pleasure. I said to her, 'Then you could see the relatives of a court noble there.' So we went there. Juzôbô (who brought those china things to me) was there and said, 'This woman had intercourse with a snake.' When I heard this, I thought that she did not mate with a snake but that she had the body of a snake. While I was thinking that, Juzôbô said, 'She is a human being and a snake at the same time.' And I awoke. After awakening, I thought that she must be Zenmyô. Zenmyô is a dragon-man and had the body of a snake, and the fact that she was of pottery means that she was petrified.

This is a fascinating dream. Myôe's love transforms a pottery figure into a real woman. The dream recalls Myôe's other dream in which a stone has an eye and moves like a living creature. In both dreams, inanimate objects become alive. In order to know the full meaning of this dream, we must know who is Zenmyô, because Myôe himself perceives the pottery woman in the dream to be Zenmyô. Zenmyô is a heroine who appears in the story of the founders of Hua-Yen. Actually, Myôe himself asks the artists to paint these stories and made "The picture stories of the founders of Hua-Yen," which is still extant even though one part is missing. Here we shall offer a summary of the stories.

10. The Picture Stories of the Founders of Hua-Yen

These are the stories about the two founders of Hua-Yen in Shiragi (a part of Korea). There are two Buddhist priests, Gengyô and Gishô. They go on a journey to China in order to learn Hua-Yen's teaching. One night they stay in a kind of cave to avoid heavy rain. In the morning they find that the cave is actually a grave. They stay there the following night as well. Then Gengyô dreams that an Oni (a kind of demon) appears to scare him. After waking, Gengyô realizes that the Oni appears only after he knows the place where he is sleeping is a grave. He recognizes that seeing an Oni depends entirely upon the situation of his psyche. Hence the most important thing is the inner psyche and not the outer world. With this insight, he decides not to go to China, nor to seek the truth in the outer world, but to go back to Korea.

When Gengyô arrives back home he drinks saké, goes to houses of prostitution, and plays musical instruments, thus transgressing the precepts. He does not care about outer things and concentrates on inner development. In due course he becomes a great priest in Korea. It was said that even wild animals became gentle when he did meditations.

In the meantime the queen becomes ill. No one can cure her. The king worries about it a great deal and sends messenger to China in order to find a remedy for the queen. When the messenger's ship is sailing to China somebody comes out of the sea and asks the messenger to follow him. The messenger is led to the Dragon Palace at the bottom of the sea. The Dragon king says to the emissary that if somebody else can preach to the people based on the holy scriptures, which he would give to the messenger, the queen would surely be cured. The emissary carries back the scriptures to the king and tells him all about it. The king makes a great effort to find a priest who can understand the holy scriptures from the Dragon Palace. Finally, Gengyô is summoned. Upon accomplishing this great task the queen is cured.

Gishô continues his journey to China even though Gengyô has returned home. One day Gishô meets a beautiful young lady called Zenmyô. She is very much attracted to him and expresses her love to him. He declines it, saying that he cannot accept it as he must keep the precepts of the Buddhist priests. Upon hearing this, Zenmyô gives up her intention and becomes quite religious. When Gishô finishes his study he wants to go back to Shiragi. Zenmyô learns of this and hurries to the harbor to see him off. She is too late. All she can see is Gishô's ship already far away on the sea. She throws her present to him into the sea hoping that it would reach him. This, however, is not enough for her. Finally she jumps into the sea and turns into a dragon. The dragon assists Gishô's ship in its return to Shiragi.

After arriving at Shiragi, Gishô tries to spread the Hua-Yen teaching. When Gishô has difficulty in getting land to build a temple Zenmyô changes from a dragon to a big stone about four kilometers long which floats in the air and scares the priests who oppose Gishô, so that he succeeds in building a temple to teach Hua-Yen. This is the end of story of Gishô. However the picture of the last part of the story, Zenmyô's becoming a big stone, is not extant although all other parts have been kept in the Kyoto national museum.

Knowing the stories, we have a much better understanding of Myôe's dream. Before going into the interpretation of the dream I would like to point out some remarkable features of the picture stories, because the characteristics of the two founders of Hua-Yen reflect much of Myôe's personality. Here the contrast between the deeds of Gengyô and Gishô is quite clear: Gengyô goes back to Korea putting an emphasis on the inner world, whereas Gishô goes to China to get the teaching from abroad. Concerning the relationship with women the contrast is also obvious: Gengyô accepts sexual relations, going into houses of prostitution, whereas Gishô rejected Zenmyô's love. In addition Gengyô rescues a woman, namely the queen, by spreading the teaching, whereas Gishô spreads the teaching by the help of a woman, namely Zenmyô. All the contrasts are shown in the following table:

Gengyô	Gishô
Goes back home (sought teaching inside)	Goes to China (sought teaching from abroad)
Acceptance of sex (has relations with prostitutes)	Rejection of sex (rejects Zenmyô's proposal)
By spreading the teaching to people, rescues a woman (the queen)	By the help of a woman (Zenmyô) spreads the teaching to the people

Figure 4. Two Founders of Hua-Yen

These remarkable contrasts reflect the strong polarities in Myôe's psyche. Myôe keeps strict celibacy, but this does not mean that he has no interest in women. One year after he had that dream, he rescues many widows and daughters of warriors and court nobles who died in the war between the emperor and the Shogun. He does it at the risk of his life. Many women worship him and put trust in him. Myôe once told his disciples that on several occasions he was tempted to have intimate relationships with women but that each time, some strange or unexpected thing happened to prevent him from doing so. His conflict regarding women is strong and takes time to overcome.

If we look at the attitude of Gengyô and Gishô towards women, we find very interesting polarities, as shown in Figure 5.

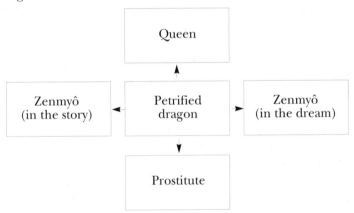

Figure 5. Female Polarities in Picture Stories of Hua-Yen

The vertical axis is that of the Mother, a queen on the top and a prostitute at the bottom. Gengyô's relation to women worked mainly on this axis. A prostitute denotes one aspect of the Mother, who "accepts" everybody without discrimination, and with whom it is easy to have bodily contact. Whereas a queen accepts everybody equally as the Mother of the country, but no one except the king can have bodily contact with her.

Crossing this vertical axis is the horizontal anima axis. At the left side I put Zenmyô in Gishô's story. She is beautiful and helpful to men but has no sexual relationships with men. The fact that the dragon of Zenmyô petrifies into stone means that her emotion is fixed at some point and is alive no more, even though her petrification helps Gishô. If we put the anima, who has sexual relations with men, on the right side of the axis, Zenmyô's move from left to right is stopped in the center by being petrified. I do not feel it to be mere chance that this part of the picture is lost when the other parts are all still extant.

If we take all these things into consideration we can understand that Myôe's deed in his dream is a great task. He gives life to the petrified anima. His saying to the woman in the dream that he is a saint sounds quite arrogant. But in view of his extraordinarily modest attitude in daily life, his words are necessary so that he might stand firm in front of the petrified anima in order to give her life.

Now we can understand that the dream in which the stone begins to move like a fish is a forerunner of this dream. The image of the decayed fish and the suffering of the creature in that dream follows along the line of his first dream (in which a woman was dismembered) and the image of decayed anima in the "Pictures of Nine Phases."

If we look at Figure 5, we see that it really reveals Myôe's way of relating to women, or his relation to the body, or even to the world, according to the Hua-Yen teaching. Gengyô's way is strictly on the vertical axis. His story shows the paradoxical nature of the axis, namely, that he can only reach the top by way of falling down to the bottom. As we know already, he does not mind having relations with prostitutes and he finally rescues the queen.

However, this is not enough. In order to have a truly individual relationship, man must have horizontal movements as well. The vertical axis is, I think, a collective one.

In contrast with Gengyô, Gishô's relation with women is quite individual. However, his task is not accomplished fully because Zenmyô is petrified. The emotion is fixed in the center of the axis, and I believe at this point there is great danger of falling down to the bottom of the collective axis. Priests in Myôe's era who have sexual relations with women easily follow this way. In this case the sexual relation does not have the meaning of the union of opposites. However, Myôe succeeds in accomplishing the task of Gishô by accepting intimate relations with a woman in the dream. He gives life to the pottery woman. The most interesting fact is that he does it by way of keeping his celibacy strictly in his outer life. This is also an important paradox. It is just like Gengyô, who reaches the top by way of falling down to the bottom. However difficult or painful it may be, one has to stay at the bottom since it appears to be the only way of reaching the top. A careless upward movement results in petrification.

11. Coagulation of the Body and of the Mind

The theme of the number two appears again and again in Myôe's dreams. We can also see strong contrasts in the stories of the two founders of Hua-Yen and Chen-Yen: I have suggested them to be the paternal and the maternal principles. However, we should say now that all the number twos in his dreams are not so simple and indicate that there are many polarities in Myôe's being.

About four months after Myôe's dream of Zenmyô, he has an extraordinary experience during a Zen meditation. He describes it in his dream diary as "a coagulation of the body and the mind." His vision is as follows:

> From the sky a hollow tube made of glass came down to me. When I took it, somebody pulled it up with me to the

sky. I thought I reached Tusita (where Maitreya gives sermons). On the top of the tube there was a precious ball.
Holy water came out from it and flowed over my whole body.
Then I wanted to see my real body. Suddenly my face became a bright mirror. It became like a crystal ball and rolled
over to another place. A voice said, 'All Buddhas now entered into it. You will change into a bigger body and be
blessed.' And I came out from the vision.

It is a superb vision. After his experience with the
dream of Zenmyô, Myôe's relation with his body must
have changed. In the vision, his body and mind coagulat-
ed like a crystal in the center of the universe. All the
Buddhas can enter into it. Now his whole being becomes
transparent, allowing others to penetrate into himself.
This is truly the highest point that one can reach according to the Hua-Yen teaching. Toshihiko Izutsu describes
it as follows:

Before, in the first Domain, all these things were dark,
opaque, and mutually obstructive. Now their material opaci-
ty is gone; luminosity and transparency take its place. And in
the universal expanse of the cosmic light, the things begin to
be interfused freely and unimpededly with one another, so
that the whole world of being appears as an intricate web of
lights mutually penetrating into one another.[1]

Myôe's vision, I think, shows that he had reached this
extreme point.

1. Toshihiko Izutsu, "The Nexus of Ontological Events," *Eranos* 48 –
1980, p. 383.

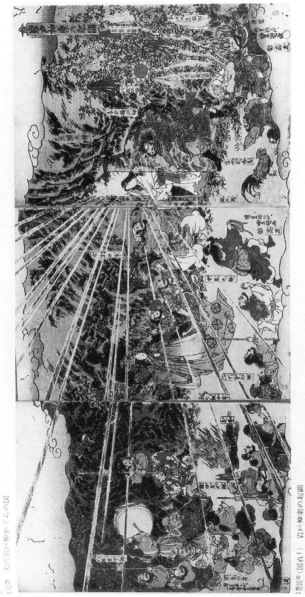

Figure 6. The Sun Goddess appearing from the rock cave

III. Japanese Mythology: Balancing the Gods

1. The Sun Goddess, Amaterasu

At first glance, one is likely to feel that the most important figure in Japanese mythology is the Sun Goddess, Amaterasu. I would like to call your attention to the fact that the sun is a goddess in Japan although in many other cultures it is presented as a male deity. In Japan it is the female sun who shines in Heaven.

The emperors of Japan are supposed to be descendents of this goddess. As it is told in the myth, the Sun Goddess who lives in Heaven finds the land of Japan so exquisite that she sends her grandson to reign over the country. His grandson, the great-great-grandson of the goddess, becomes the first emperor of Japan.

Before going on to relate the stories about this Great Goddess, I would like to mention that there are two main sources of Japanese mythology, the *Kojiki (The Records of Ancient Things)* and the *Nihonshoki (The Chronicles of Japan)*, otherwise known as the *Nihongi*.[1] Both are written at the beginning of the 8th Century and contain not only myths and legends but the records of actual historical events as well. They are also written with political motives in mind: first, to demonstrate that the emperor is a descendant of a god and had attained superiority over other tribes in Japan; and second, especially the *Nihonshoki*, to assert the independence and autonomy of the Japanese

---

1. Translations in the present article are mine. Both works exist in English translation: *Kojiki,* trans. with an Introduction and Notes by Donald L. Philippi, Tokyo and Princeton 1969; *Nihongi: Chronicals of Japan from the Earliest Times to A.D. 679,* trans. by W. G. Aston, London 1956.

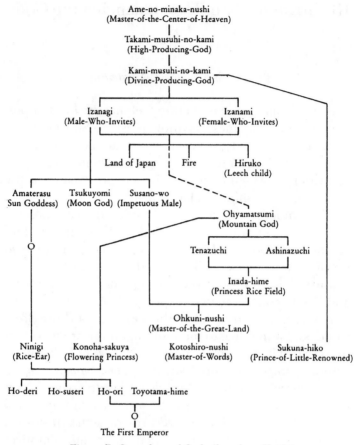

Figure 7. Genealogy of Gods (based on Kojiki)

nation in the international arena. In this sense the *Nihon-shoki* is closely modelled after Chinese chronicles; it has a rationale at its basis and is written with the intention of establishing an official chronicle of the nation. Though these political aspects are extraneous to our interests, the *Nihonshoki* is nevertheless an extremely valuable source insofar as it provides us with many different versions of mythological episodes. Comparisons between the *Nihon-shoki*, the *Kojiki,* and other versions will give us interesting clues to an understanding of the mythology. My presentation is based primarily on the *Kojiki* because I feel that the accounts it contains are closest to the original indigenous Japanese mythos.

It is said in the *Kojiki* that the Sun Goddess is born from her father's left eye after her mother dies. She is "the father's daughter," just as Kerényi tells us concerning Pallas Athene that "at her birth the father played a more important role than the mother."[1] The Sun Goddess' father, Izanagi (Male-Who-Invites) has just come back from the underworld. He had gone there to fetch his wife, Izanami (Female-Who-Invites), who died giving birth to the fire god. He failed to bring her back. But because he has been in a polluted land he must purify himself. Entering a river for the purification, he says, "The current is too rapid in the upper reaches and too weak in the lower." So he only goes into the middle area. Three major gods are born out of the defiled Land of Gloom during this purification process. Izanagi purifies his left eye and gives birth to the Sun Goddess, Amaterasu. The Moon God, Tsukiyomi comes from the right eye. And Susano-wo, the Storm God comes from the nose. Izanagi rejoices and says, "I have had child after child and have finally given birth to the three most noble." He then gives an order to the Sun Goddess to reign over Takama-no-hara (The Plains of High Heaven). Izanagi instructs the Moon God and the Storm God to reign over the Land of Night and over the Domain of the Seas, respectively.

The *Nihonshoki* gives a different version of this episode. After Izanagi and Izanami give birth to all the islands of Japan and to other lesser gods, they consult each other

1. Karl Kerényi, *The Gods of the Greeks,* Thames and Hudson, London 1951, p. 120.

on the matter of producing someone who will be the Lord of the Universe. Then they give birth to the Sun Goddess, who is named Oho-hiru-meno-muchi (Great-Noon-Female). The parents rejoice and decide to send her to Heaven. Then they produce the Moon God and send him to Heaven to be the consort of the Sun Goddess. Next to be born is Hiruko, the Leech Child. Because he cannot stand upright even at the age of three, his parents put him in Ame-no-Iwakusu-Fune (Heavenly-Rock-Camphor-Wood-Boat) and abandon him to the winds. Last to be born is Susano-wo, the Storm God.

2. The Counterpart of the Sun Goddess, Susano-Wo

The Storm God does not accept the task which his father Izanagi assigns to him and simply cries and cries until his beard reaches his breast. Finally his father asks him why he is weeping so incessantly. The Storm God answers that he is crying because he wishes to visit his mother in the Land of Gloom. It is interesting to note that the Storm God is a mother-bound child, contrary to his sister, the Sun Goddess, who is a father's daughter. The father god, who has already divorced his wife, is furious to hear what his son has to say. Izanagi says to him, "You shall not remain in this land."

The Storm God wants to visit his sister Amaterasu in Heaven to say goodbye to her. The Sun Goddess is surprised to hear the groaning of the mountains and rivers, which is caused by the Storm God's approach. She misunderstands his visit and thinks that her brother is coming to Heaven with the evil intention of taking over her land. It is important to note here that the Sun Goddess makes a mistake; she is not a supreme and righteous god.

Preparing for confrontation with the Storm God, she changes her hair-do into that of a man. She carries thousands of arrows and a bow, stands her ground with dignity and utters a mighty cry of defiance. We can see how similar the Sun Goddess is to Pallas Athene, who was born wearing an armor of gleaming gold and uttering a far-reaching battle cry. When the Storm God meets his sister, he reassures her by explaining the situation. She is rather suspicious, however, and asks him for some proof of his truthfulness. Her brother suggests that the two of them should make an oath and produce children.

The Sun Goddess and the Storm God make their oath to each other from the opposite banks of the River of Heaven. The Goddess asks the Storm God for his sword, named "the Sword of Ten Grasps" because it is so long. She breaks it into three pieces and rinses them in the sacred Well of Heaven. She chews them up and exhales a mist out of which three goddesses come into being. The Storm God then asks his sister for the curved jewels which are entwined in her hair on the left side. He rinses them in the Well of Heaven, chews them and exhales a mist, whence comes the god who is the ancestor of the Japanese emperor. The Storm God takes the other jewels belonging to the Sun Goddess and in the same manner creates a total of five gods.

The Great Goddess says that the five boys are hers because they were born from her belongings and that the three girls are his since they came into being from his property. However, the Storm God, also known as the Impetuous Male, then says that he proved the purity of his heart by begetting girls. He declares, "Naturally, I won!" The facts to which we must pay attention are, firstly, the Storm God's defeat of the Sun Goddess, and secondly, a higher value given to female, rather than male, offspring.

This is a point which even the ancient Japanese must have had difficulty in understanding, as we can see from the fact that there are numerous variations of this episode. The *Nihonshoki* tells us the same story as the *Kojiki*, but does not always say who wins the contest. In one version of the *Nihonshoki*, however, the Storm God wins, and the reason given is that he has begotten males instead of females.

After the birth of the children, all versions agree that the five boys are kept in Heaven and the three girls are sent down to Earth, or more precisely, to the land of Japan. The three female deities can be found even today at the Munakata shrine in Kyushu. They are the goddesses of navigation. The five male deities are said to be the ancestors of the main tribes of ancient Japan, one of them being the progenitor of the Japanese Emperor.

When the Storm God comes to bid her farewell, she misunderstands his intent and is defeated by her brother in a contest. Upon winning the contest, the Storm God becomes violent in the joy of victory. His sister does not become angry, but instead tries to justify her brother's violent acts. Here we are impressed with the female quality of the Sun Goddess, especially if we recall her former attitude in confronting the Storm God. In spite of her generous excuses on his behalf, his evil acts become ever more flagrant. He flays a piebald horse and throws it down into the Sun Goddess' sacred weaving hall, tearing off its roof. A maiden weaver who is working with the great goddess is struck and fatally wounded in her genitals by a weaving shuttle. Terrified at the sight of his violence, the goddess retires into the Stone Cavern of Heaven. According to the *Nihonshoki*, it is the Sun Goddess herself who, stirred with alarm, wounds herself with the weaving shuttle, though not fatally. In another version, it is said that a goddess named Waka-Hiru-Me (Young-

Noon-Female) dies. She is said to be a younger sister or a daughter of the Sun Goddess. Waka-Hiru-me may thus refer ultimately to either the Sun Goddess herself or the maiden image of the Sun Goddess.

3. The Retirement of the Sun Goddess

When the Sun Goddess hides herself in the Stone Cavern of Heaven, darkness descends upon heaven and earth. It is perpetually night, and the world is filled with evil. All the eight hundred myriad gods assemble and seek a plan which will entice the goddess from out of her hiding place. The goddess Ame-no-Uzume (Heavenly-Frightening-Female) performs a dance in front of the door of the Stone Cavern. In the course of her dance she tugs at the nipples of her breasts and pulls down her skirt, exposing her genitals to the gods who gathered around her. The eight hundred myriad gods break out laughing, whereupon the Great Goddess peeps out of her cave and warily asks why they are laughing so joyfully. Ame-no-Uzume lies saying, "All the gods are pleased because a goddess who is nobler than the Great Goddess herself has appeared." The Sun Goddess feels quite strange, because she in fact did see the face of a beautiful goddess. This was nothing more than a reflection of herself in a mirror held up to her face by the gods. In this way she is successfully lured out of the cave. The mirror used in this ritual is the chief object of worship at the Great Shrine at Ise which is dedicated to the Sun Goddess and is the highest shrine in Japan.

In one version of the *Nihonshoki,* it is stated that the mirror is placed in the cave. When the goddess comes out, it is slightly damaged as it strikes against the door. The flaw is said to remain to this day. This suggests that the people of ancient Japan suspected some imperfections in the image of their highest deity. Or we might say that the image of the sun must contain some shadows in order to be complete.

This story of the Sun Goddess and the Storm God calls to mind the story of Persephone and Hades in Greek mythology. In the former, the Storm God alarms his sister by throwing a horse down into her sacred weaving hall while she is weaving. In the latter, Hades ravishes the maiden Persephone with his immortal steed while she is gathering flowers in a meadow. In the Japanese myth, the male intruder is not astride a horse but throws one. In either case, the instinctual aspect of the masculine is expressed in the presence of the horse. However, with regard to the expression of the feminine aspect, we find that in the Japanese myth, the distinction between the mother and daughter is not so clearly delineated as it is in the Greek myth, wherein the figure of Demeter is clearly distinct from that of her daughter Persephone. In one version, we are told that Waka-Hiru-Me (Young-Noon-Female) mortally wounds herself with a weaving shuttle which she holds in her hand. She is said to be the Sun Goddess's younger sister or daughter. It is through the intrusion of the Storm God upon the virgin figure of the Sun Goddess as Waka-Hiru-Me that the Sun Goddess experiences her male counterpart. The Sun Goddess is simultaneously Persephone, Demeter who laments her daughter, as well as the observer Helios. This raises the question as to who takes the role of Zeus. In the story of Demeter and Hades, Zeus plays the role of the mediator, but the Sun Goddess does not take such a clearly neutral position. I am led to the rather strange conclusion that it is the Moon God, the other member belonging to the three most noble offspring of Izanagi, who must correspond to Zeus. The Moon God exists in the center, but is not necessarily the mightiest. The one who stands in the center and sees the intense conflict between the siblings does nothing, thus requiring the combined efforts of the eight hundred myriad gods to solve the problem.

The enticing ritual dance performed by Heavenly-Frightening-Female and the use of the sacred mirror is similar to the Baubo incident in Greek mythology. Their deeds provoke a smile and laughter respectively. In the Greek myth Demeter smiles, while in the Japanese myth the myriad gods burst into laughter. This laughter helps release the tension and opens up a previously unseen path of resolution. Heavenly-Frightening-Female's answer to the Sun Goddess's question concerning the source of the laughter is quite revealing. The former replies that a goddess nobler than the Sun Goddess herself has appeared. Yet this was nothing more than a reflection of her image in the sacred mirror. Among the many symbolic meanings attributable to the mirror, the one which is revealed by the etymology seems to be most applicable here. "Kagami," the Japanese word for mirror, stems from "kage-mi," where "kage" means reflection or shadow and "mi" means "to see." The Sun Goddess must face, be surprised, and accept her reflected image, the dark side of the spiritual virgin. From this we can see that Heavenly-Frightening-Female who performs the "indecent" dance is actually an aspect of the Sun Goddess herself.

4. The Moon God as the Hollow Center

After the Sun Goddess' appearance, all the gods form a council and demand a heavy fine from the Storm God. The god is not executed; instead his beard and finger nails are cut and he is expelled from Heaven. However, this is by no means the end of the Storm God. He descends to Japan and re-emerges as a cultural hero in the Land of Izumo.

When the Storm God descends to Izumo, he encounters an old couple and their daughter, all of whom he finds crying. He asks them about the cause of their sorrow, whereupon an old earthly deity explains that a big serpent named Yamata-no-Orochi (Eight-Tailed-Serpent) has been coming once a year to devour the old couple's daughters. They had eight daughters but now only one remains, Kushinada-Hime (otherwise known as Inada-Hime). The Storm God rescues the maiden by slaying the dragon after tricking it into getting drunk on a huge amount of sake (rice wine). The Storm God eventually marries the maiden. Considering what has been written about the Storm God in Japanese mythology, one cannot say that he is clearly evil or bad. His character is somewhat like that of Set in Egyptian mythology, who is also a storm god. There are important differences, however. The Sun Goddess and Storm God fight each other but neither one is clearly right or wrong. Neither death nor dismemberment occur as a result of the conflict. The Storm God is not the enemy of the Sun Goddess but a subtle counterpart.

As I said earlier, the god Izanagi gave birth to the three most noble gods, the Sun Goddess, the Moon God, and the Storm God. It seems quite strange that there is nothing concerning the Moon God in the *Kojiki,* in contrast to the other two who are highly visible and active. In the *Nihonshoki* as well, little is said about the Moon God. The complete negation of the Moon God appears even more curious when we recall that the Japanese have had a deep appreciation of the moon from ancient times. If you read the oldest collection of poetry, the Manyoshu, you will find many poems about the moon but very few referring to the sun. I wondered why the Moon God was so completely neglected in Japanese mythology, and came to the rather peculiar conclusion that the Moon God was highly valued, but by carrying out the paradoxical role of standing at the center of the pantheon and doing nothing. One of the reasons for this conclusion is that neither of the other two of the triad, the Sun Goddess and the Storm God, can be made to conform to the role of the central deity in the Japanese pantheon. Upon initial encounter, the Sun Goddess seems to be the central figure, but upon closer scrutiny, we see that such is not the case.

The Sun Goddess reigns over the Plains of High Heaven. But when the Storm God comes to bid her farewell, and she misunderstands his intent and is defeated by her brother in contest, it shows that even the Sun Goddess will fail if she thinks of herself as being the center. The Storm God proves to be a failure at center as well when he rejoices as the victor of their contest. Each effectively counters the other, forming a subtle balance. But in the midst of their interplay, the center is actually occupied by the Moon God who does not do anything.

The idea of placing the Moon God in the center is also supported by the fact that we can find other similar kinds of triads in the *Kojiki*.

5. The First and Third Triads

According to the *Kojiki,* the first important triad appeared in the beginning of the world. There are several different versions of the Japanese creation myth, some of which are clearly influenced by Chinese culture. Although a comparison between the various descriptions of the beginning of the world would be interesting, here I remain content to give the version contained in the *Koji-*

ki. At the beginning of this work we are given the names
of the deities that were born in the Plains of High Heaven
when heaven and earth were first established. They are
Ame-no-Minaka-Nushi-no-Kami (Master-of-the-Center-of-
Heaven), Takami-Musuhi-no Kami (High-Producing-
God), and Kami-Musuhi-no-Kami (Divine-Producing-
God). These three are all born spontaneously and hide
themselves.

The first god, whose name actually tells us that he is at
the center, never appears in the mythology again, while
the other two play important roles. The difference between these latter two is clear. Anesaki, a Japanese scholar
of religion, has gone so far as to denote the gender of
these two gods when he translated their names into English, even though no such information is directly given
in the mythological accounts. He refers to them as High-
Producing-God and Divine-Producing-Goddess. In any
case, it is obvious that the former expresses the male principle and the latter the female principle. High-Producing-God is also called High-Tree-God and is always standing beside the Sun Goddess as if he were a protective
father. The Sun Goddess' favorite son marries one of
High-Producing-God's daughters, and the son born from
this marriage descends to the Land of Japan to reign over
it. High-Producing-God is really the god of production on
the high plains.

The first triad, born at the begin-ning of the world	Takami-musuhi-no-kami High Pro-ducing God (Paternal Principle)	Ameno-minaka-nushi Master-of-the-Center-of-Heaven (The Cen-ter)	Kami-musuhi-no-kami Divine Pro-ducing God (Maternal Principle)	Birth by themselves

The second triad, born at the first contact between Heaven and Underworld	Amaterasu (Sun Goddess)	Tsukiyomi (Moon Goddess)	Susanowo (Storm God)	Birth from their father in the water
The third triad, born of the first marriage between a heavenly deity and an earthly deity	Hoderi Fire Radiant Lord Sea-luck-lad	Hosuseri Fire Raging Lord	Hoori Fire Bending Lord Mountain luck-lad	Birth from their mother in the fire

Figure 8. The Three Important Triads in Japanese Mythology

Opposed to this we have the Divine-Producing-God, who is closely associated with the Storm God and the land he reigned over after he was expelled from Heaven. Few of Divine-Producing-God's deeds are mentioned in the official mythology of the *Nihonshoki*. However, many of his activities are described in the *Kojiki* and *Izumo Fudoki* *(Ancient Records of the History and Geography of the Izumo area)*. He is a miraculous healer and resuscitated one of the most important sons of the Storm god, Ohkuni-nushi (Master of the Great Land) who had been burned to death.

Whereas High-Producing-God is concerned with production in Heaven, Divine-Producing-God is related to Earth, and Master-of-the-Center-of-Heaven exists in between them as the center which does nothing. The first generation triad has, as we can see, a similar structure to the second one: the Sun Goddess, the Moon God, and the Storm God.

Now I would like to mention the third triad. In Japanese mythology one can find many similar events which are variations of a single theme with only subtle differences. The birth of the third triad is one such event. The grandson of the Sun Goddess Ninigi takes over Japan. One day he meets a beautiful girl named Konohana-no-Sakuya-Hime (Flowering Princess), a daughter of the Mountain God. As it must be apparent by now, the coexistence of heavenly and earthly gods is quite standard in Japanese mythology. Konohana-no-Sakuya-Hime is an earthly goddess to whom Ninigi, a heavenly god, proposes. The princess replies that she first has to consult her father. Her father is pleased to hear about Ninigi's proposal to his daughter. So he sends her together with her daughter Iwa-Naga-Hime (Rock-Long-Princess) to live with him. However, the heavenly god accepts only the Flowering Princess and rejects Rock-Long-Princess since the latter is terribly ugly. Rock-Long-Princess returns to her home, and her father tells her that Ninigi will not live very long because he has rejected her. One night, Ninigi makes love to Flowering Princess. Sometime thereafter, she tells him that she is going to give birth to his child. He can not believe this because they had only slept together once. In order to prove that he is actually the father she gives birth in a burning house saying, "Unless he is divine, he will certainly die." The child, born in the midst of the blazing fire, is named Ho-deri (Radiant Fire Lord). He is followed by two others, Ho-suseri (Raging Fire Lord) and Ho-ori (Bending Fire Lord). They comprise the third triad and are the first offspring to be born as a result of the marriage between a heavenly deity and an earthly one. The episode with Rock-Long-Princess suggests that Ninigi and his offspring cannot be immortal although they can still be said to belong among the heavenly gods.

I would like briefly to relate some stories about the third triad. Another name for the first born, Ho-deri, is Sea-Luck-Lad because he is a fisherman. The third, Ho-ori, is also called Mountain-Luck-Lad because he hunts birds and animals in the mountains. One day Mountain-Luck-Lad asks his brother to exchange roles. He fishes all day long, but in vain. He even loses the fishing hook that he had borrowed from his brother. Sea-Luck-Lad is furious when he finds out and insists on getting the hook back. Mountain-Luck-Lad goes down to the palace of the Sea God to look for it. There he meets a beautiful princess named Toyotama-Hime and marries her. One day, after having been in the depths of the sea for three years, he heaves a great sigh. His wife asks what troubles him, whereupon he tells her of his troubles with his brother. Through the help of her father, the Sea God, Mountain-Luck-Lad is able to recover the hook. He rises up from the sea, goes ashore, returns the hook to his brother, and then tortures him with some magic balls he has received from the Sea God until Sea-Luck-Lad surrenders completely. Later on, a child of Mountain-Luck-Lad and Toyotama-Hime becomes the father of the first emperor of Japan.

In this story the first and third brothers play important roles, but again there is no mention of the second brother, Ho-suseri. Just as in the first two triads, the center, in this case Ho-suseri, does nothing. I have named this structure, in which the center does not do anything, the Hollow Center Structure of Japanese Mythology.

6. The Repetition of Balancing Movements

Throughout the mythology of Japan, one is impressed by the fact that a basic story is retold again and again with only subtle changes. I feel that this is indicative of an attempt to maintain a fine balance between various pairs of opposites. This occurs throughout the historical periods described in the *Kojiki*. One can say that this continues in Japan even today. But before going on to examine the contemporary situation, I would like to present some examples from the *Kojiki*.

The conflict between the Sun Goddess and the Storm God is actually a kind of repetition of the drama which unfolded between their parents. Their mother, Izanami, dies in the fire to which she herself had given birth. Their father, Izanagi, goes down to the underworld to bring her back, but when he meets his wife she asks him not to look at her while she is negotiating with the gods of the underworld. In spite of the promise which he made to her, he lights up the darkness of the underworld. He then sees that his wife is in a horrible state of disintegration – her body being infected with maggots and eight thundergods swarming within her. Frightened at the sight, he flees. His wife, who was also his sister, is enraged at being seen in such a shameful state and pursues him with the help of some old hags from the Land of Gloom.

The conflict between sister and brother, Izanami and Izanagi, carries over into the second generation of the Sun Goddess and the Storm God. This time, however, it is the male, the Storm God, who is violent. We can see that the roles of the sexes have been reversed. Whereas the male god Izanagi flees having seen the terrible state of his wife's body, the female deity, the Sun Goddess, retires into a cave upon seeing her brother's violent acts. It is highly significant that the same word is used in the *Kojiki* to describe the reaction of both Izanagi and the Sun Goddess to the sight which repels them. It is *kashikomi*, which means roughly "to be awed." First Izanagi is awed by the truth which appeared out of the depths of female being.

His daughter is in turn stricken with the same feeling of awe in confronting the strong violence lying at the depths of the male. In this way, the opposing pair of male and female balance each other.

After their confrontations, the respective pairs achieve a kind of balance. In the continuation of the first story, Izanami pursues her husband-brother to the pass leading from this world to the Land of Gloom and tells him that she will kill a thousand inhabitants of his land every day. To this he replies that he will build fifteen hundred child-bearing huts every day. Here we see a rather primitive and naive form of compromise.

In the case of the Sun Goddess and the Storm God, a much longer period is required to reach a resolution, but as we shall see, balance is achieved through true compromise. It may be recalled that the myriad gods punish the Storm God and expel him from Heaven after the Sun Goddess comes out of the Stone Cavern. It is obvious that no compromise is made at this point. But then the Storm God descends to Izumo (a district in Japan) and slays the Eight-tailed Serpent. After he slays it, he finds a sword in the middle tail. His next act is quite unexpected. He makes a gift of the sword to his sister, the Sun Goddess in Heaven. The presentation of the precious object to the sister who expelled him constitutes a compromise on the part of the Storm God. This deed is especially noteworthy if we recall that the Great Goddess was already armed with bow and arrow at the time of her confrontation with her brother, but not with a sword, which has the function of cutting. The Storm God may think that it is necessary for his sister to make a cut.

To the contrary, the act of giving the sword foreshadows a still greater compromise between the two of them which takes place when the Sun Goddess wishes to acquire the land over which her brother reigns. She tries to send her grandson to the land ruled by the son of the Storm God, Ohkuni-Nushi (Master of the Great Land). This is not an easy thing to do, and there are some troubles within both parties. Finally, however, they are able to agree that the grandson from Heaven will take over the land under the condition that a large shrine would be built for the Master of the Great Land. Furthermore, it is decided that the heavenly gods would have control over public affairs while the earthly gods would rule over divine affairs. All of this constitutes a major compromise on the part of everyone concerned, between female and male, Heaven and Earth, above and below. Yet it is a more or less a repetition of the action of the prior generation, the parents, albeit on a larger and more peaceable scale.

I would like to point out the fact that these kinds of repetitive balancing movements take place many times during the actual history of Japan as given by the *Kojiki*. Even though the emperors, the descendants of the Sun Goddess, take the central role in Japan politically, balancing movements are repeatedly required due to actions on the part of the Storm God. For example, the prince of the eleventh Emperor Suinin, named Homuchi-Wake, does not say anything even though his beard becomes so long that it reaches down to his chest. This is reminiscent of the time when the Storm God's beard similarly grew down to his chest as he cried longingly for his mother. Prince Homuchi-Wake's mother dies just after his birth in the midst of a sister-brother conflict. His father, the Emperor, is worried about his son's mutism. One night, a god appears in his dream and tells him that his son will begin to speak if a shrine is built for the god as splendid as the palace of the Emperor. Upon awakening, the Emperor realizes that the god was Ohkuni-Nushi, the son of the Storm God. So he sends his son along with a retinue to Izumo where Ohkuni-Nushi's shrine is located. The

Emperor is delighted to find Homuchi-Wake actually speaking when he visits the Izumo Shrine. This event shows the importance of the Izumo Shrine with respect to the Imperial family. The descendants of the Sun Goddess are made to recall the existence of the descendants of the Storm God by the force of the latter's magical powers.

The next episode in the *Kojiki is* of interest to us as well. On the way home from his trip to Izumo, Homuchi-Wake meets Princess Hinaga and marries her. But when he peers into her room, he sees that she is actually a large serpent. He is horrified and flees immediately. The princess pursues him over the high seas. The prince is frightened and tells his retinue to pull his ship up a mountain in order to escape the serpent. Atsuhiko Yoshida, a Japanese scholar of mythology, points out an important feature of this event.[1] After agreeing with my theory that an hollow center structure lies at the basis of Japanese mythology, he says that this episode concerning Homuchi-Wake is the exact reversal of the episode of the Storm God's conquest of the Eight-tailed Serpent. The Prince becomes aware of the serpentine aspect of the feminine only after he marries the maiden. As soon as he sees this aspect, he runs away from her without any thought of confrontation. This is just the opposite of the Storm God's actions. He slays the Eight-tailed Serpent and then marries the maiden, who would otherwise have fallen victim to the serpent. Homuchi-Wake's actions have a twofold significance: First he shows the necessity of worshipping the Storm God's son, and second, he tries to nullify the Storm God's heroic deed by doing the exact opposite of his predecessor.

The power of the Sun Goddess counteracts the power of the Storm God. The Storm God's conquest of the ser-

1. Atsuhiko Yoshida, "Susano-wo Shinwa to Homuchiwake-Yamato-takeru Densetsu," *Gendai Shiso*, Vol. 10, No. 12., Seidosha 1982.

pent and his subsequent marriage is then erased by Homuchi-Wake. In the course of studying Japanese fairy
tales, I began to wonder why we don't have the story of
the so-called "dragon fight" as it appears in the West. This
is all the more peculiar in light of the fact that we do have
the Storm God's fight with the serpent. I have a deep
interest in this matter because Erich Neumann has taken
up the "dragon fight" as an archetypal pattern underlying
the establishment of modern Western consciousness. At
first I had thought that the Storm God was a hidden deity
overshadowed by the brilliance of the female sun who
occupies the highest position in the Japanese mythological hierarchy. Actually, however, the two exist in an almost even balance. The Storm God reasserts himself by
slaying the Eight-tailed Serpent. He is then counterbal-
anced by Homuchi-Wake, not the Sun Goddess. This
leads us to the realization that it is the Moon God who is
the hidden one, even though he does not do anything to
affect the relationship of the two others.

7. The Hollow Center Structure

Japanese mythology, as given in the *Kojiki,* reveals a
hollow-center structure. In the diagram of "The Three
Important Triads in Japanese Mythology," the three triads are beautifully arranged and maintain a harmonious
balance. They all have one factor in common: the god
who does nothing is in the center. The triads come into
being from different conditions. The first triad appears at
the beginning of the world and is born of itself, having no
parents. The second triad is born through the first contact between Heaven and the Underworld, having
emerged from their father after he purifies himself in
water. The third triad comes into being as a result of the

first marriage between a heavenly deity and an earthly deity, and emerges from their mother in the midst of a blazing fire. The difference in birth conditions is clearly apparent. The pairs of opposites expressed within the triads are also varied. The first contains the paternal and maternal principles, the second, female and male, heaven and earth, and the third, mountain and sea.

In terms of all three triads, we can see that the center of the Japanese pantheon is occupied by the god of emptiness, respectively named Master-of-the-Center-of-Heaven, Moon God, and Raging Fire God in accordance with the type of pair of opposites at work. All the gods move and even fight one another around the hollow center. The most important thing is how well they are balanced, not victory and the acquisition of central power. This is the cosmology of the ancient Japanese and stands in distinct contrast to the structure of Christian mythology. In Christianity, a single God who is the mightiest and always right stands in the center and rules the universe. The distinction between good and evil is extremely clearcut in contrast to the amorphous nature of Japanese mythology. In Christian mythology, all elements that are not consistent with the existence of a single central deity are either banished to the periphery or completely liquidated. Quite to the contrary, in the Japanese hollow center balanced structure, even contradictory elements can co-exist so long as they can maintain a balance amongst themselves. In Christianity, the center has the power to integrate all elements whereas in Japanese mythology the center has no power.

What I would like to point out is that this hollow center balanced model is still at work in contemporary Japan. The biggest drawback of this model is the fact that the center is so weak that any element can invade it with ease. When the entire structure is kept in balance, the strength of the whole works to protect the center, but the slightest deterioration of the overall balance can result in the invasion of the center by any strong element, no matter how evil it may be. Take, for example, the case of the Sun Goddess and the Storm God. When the Sun Goddess believes that she is right and her brother wrong, she stands her ground directly in the center. This situation does not last long, however, since the Storm God takes her place after winning the contest. As soon as the Storm God feels he is in the center, the whole balance of the universe is destroyed, causing the Sun Goddess to retire into the cave. Consequently, the effort of all the gods is required to restore the balance of the universe.

The Japanese emperor is said to be a descendant of the Sun Goddess, but actually possesses the quality of the Moon God in his capacity as the center of the people. One might say that the light of the moon comes to be included in the sun when the sacred mirror is slightly damaged. This may be the significance of the female sun. It has been the role of the Emperor to stand in the center as the symbol of emptiness. Throughout its history, we find that Japan is in turmoil whenever an emperor tries to exert his power to gain control over others. We will be able to understand the significance of not only the emperor but many other phenomena in Japan as well when they are seen in terms of the hollow center balanced model.

I have said that this model can accommodate even contradictory elements. However this does not mean that the Japanese pantheon accepts everything. There is one god who was in fact rejected.

8. The Discarded God, Hiruko

In the beginning of the world as depicted in the *Nihon-shokia* strange god named Hiruko (Leech Child) is the only one not retained by the Japanese pantheon. The *Kojiki* tells us about his birth. The Celestial Divinities order Izanagi and Izanami to make the floating land firm. The two gods stand together on the floating bridge of Heaven and stir the ocean with a heavenly spear which is provided by the Celestial Divinities. When they withdraw the spear, drops fall into the ocean and become the Island of Onogoro (Self-coagulating Island). They descend to the island and create the Great Pillar of Heaven.

Izanagi and Izanami then engage in a kind of marriage ceremony. At Izanagi's suggestion, Izanami, also known as the Female-Who-Invites, starts to circumambulate the heavenly pillar from the right. Her spouse, also known as Male-Who-Invites, does the same but from the left. When they meet, the female deity exclaims, "Oh! What a lovely man!" and the male deity cries out, "Oh! What a lovely woman!" But later Male-Who-Invites says to his sister-wife, "It was not good that the woman spoke first." Consequently they beget a child of ill-fortune who cannot stand erect. He is named Hiruko (Leech Child) and is set adrift in a box made of reeds.

Worried about their failure, the two of them go up to Heaven to consult the Celestial Divinities. The deities tell the couple that it was indeed improper for the woman to have spoken first and that they had better repeat the ceremony with the error corrected. When the couple follow these instructions, they beget eight big islands, which constitute the main parts of Japan.

We can see that this account of Hiruko's birth is completely different from that of the *Nihonshoki* which I related earlier. There is another version in the *Nihonshoki*, however, which is almost identical to the one just given. In this alternate version, the same marriage ceremony takes place and is repeated to correct an error. In this version, however, the female deity initially circumambulates from the left and the male deity from the right. In the corrected ceremony, the directions are reversed. Thus there is some confusion as to the priority concerning left and right. Both the *Kojiki* and *Nihonshoki* versions agree, however, that it is not good for the female to lead the male. Please make note of this fact, since it will help us later on in resolving the fate of the unlucky child after he was set adrift in the reed box.

The story of Hiruko recalls some parallels, such as Moses in his reed box, Sargon of the Acadian myth, the lame undeveloped child of Egypt, Harpocrates (Horus the child), and Agdistis the unlucky child of a strange marriage. Some of them, as we know, return to this world with great success. Our Leech Child, however, does not return. No further mention is made of him in either the *Kojiki* or *Nihonshoki*. It is quite notable that the Japanese pantheon, which seemed to be open to any deity, could not accept this infant god.

Thus we must face the question of Hiruko's significance. There are some clues to be found in the *Kojiki's* and *Nihonshoki's* description of his birth. First, the latter tells us that Hiruko must be regarded as belonging with the Three Most Noble, namely the Sun Goddess, the Moon God, and the Storm God. Second, he may be expressive of the male sun aspect. His name, Hiruko, may mean either "Leech Child" or "Noon Child." If taken in the latter sense, he may be seen as the counterpart to Oh-Hiru-Me (Great-Noon-Female), who is really the maiden form of the Sun Goddess. We now have the interesting quaternion of the Sun Goddess, the Moon God, the Storm God, and Hiruko, the male sun. It was necessary for the Japanese pantheon to discard this last element in order to maintain the stability of its hollow center balanced structure. Japanese mythology allows for the male-female pair of opposites, but the male aspect is always softened, as expressed by the image of the female sun or the Sun Goddess in whom the light of the moon is reflected. The male sun is too strong and willful, and would disrupt the balance of the hollow center structure.

It may be recalled that Hiruko, a male deity, is born when the female deity speaks first. Later on, in the contest between the Sun Goddess and the Storm God, female offspring are valued more highly than male ones. Then the male offspring are kept in Heaven, and one of them goes on to become the ancestor of the Japanese emperor. Thus the male and female aspects continually balance each other. It might be argued that since his mother speaks first in the marriage ceremony and thus manifests the female aspect, Hiruko should have been saved as a male counterbalance. However, Hiruko rejects this kind of maneuver, since it is the very nature of the male sun to stand in the center as the mightiest one of all, spurning any kind of balancing activity. Such a god can never be accepted in the Japanese pantheon even though it is receptive to a multitude of deities. Thus Hiruko has to be sent out to sea.

It is interesting to remark how some Japanese scholars have interpreted the image of Hiruko. One said that he must be an evil spirit, while another has taken the opposite view that he is the great god who would give the whole of Japan a new orientation. These projected images are partially applicable insofar as they both express aspects of Hiruko. He appears evil from the standpoint of the Moon God. At the same time, he may be regarded as a completely new element which could open a new way for the Japanese to proceed.

This quartanio is reminiscent of what Jung said about the Trinity and the Fourth in Christianity: in the West the Fourth is female, while in Japan it is male.

This observation leads us to the conclusion that the acceptance of the strong male, which the Japanese have rejected up to now, is the onus of the modern Japanese. In mythological terms the dilemma is to find a place in the Japanese pantheon for the male sun, Hiruko. This is an extremely difficult but necessary undertaking which confronts us today. The resolution of this problem is an urgent matter in this closely knit world where the relations among many different cultures are becoming ever more intimate.

9. The Return of the Discarded Child

Even though nothing further is to be found in the official mythology, there remains the possibility of uncovering allusions to Hiruko's return in legends and fairy tales. This has long been a source of stimulation for the imagination of the Japanese.

Atsutane Hirata, a famous scholar of the Tokugawa Period (1603-1867), identified him with Sukuna-hiko (Prince-Little-Renowned), a dwarf god who comes to Izumo from the ocean in a tiny boat. Regardless of the validity of this interpretation, it remains quite interesting on the psychological level. The appearance of this prince in the *Kojiki* is quite dramatic. Once when the Master-of-the-Great-Land, the son of the Storm God, is standing on the shores of his land of Izumo, a little dwarf-like god comes ashore riding in a tiny boat made of the rind of kagami, a kind of plant, and dressed in the skin of a moth. Nobody knows who he is. A toad suggests that they ask the God of the Scarecrows, who in turn answers that the dwarf god is one of Divine-Producing-God's sons. In response to the queries of the gods in Izumo, Divine-Producing-God says, "This is indeed my child. Of all my children he is the only one who dropped down among the folk of my land." Later on Prince-Little-Renowned and Master-of-the-Great-Land become fast friends and work together to cultivate the Land of Izumo. There are many tales about his deeds in the local legends. He is a gifted healer, a cheerful character, and proves to be helpful to the Great God, Ohkuni-Nushi, who is quite a serious fellow.

Hirata's interpretation of Hiruko gives us the image of a crippled child who drifts out to sea, only to come back as a dwarf god who contributes to the establishment of the land belonging to the Storm God. I am disappointed that I cannot trace the male sun quality in him. He might have lost it or completely concealed this aspect in order to adapt to Japan.

There is another interesting identification of Hiruko with the God Ebisu, one of the Seven Deities of Good Fortune, who originates in Chinese culture. In his right hand, Ebisu carries a fishing rod and under the other hand, a sea-beam, which is regarded as a symbol of good luck. At first he was a patron of fishermen, but is now worshipped by merchants as the deity of wealth. The identification of Hiruko with Ebisu is mentioned in the literature as early as the twelfth century but it is hard to say exactly when and how this occurred. There is another deity called Ichi-gami (The God of Merchants) who is also identified with Hiruko. It is notable that Hiruko is connected with merchandise here as well. There is a folk belief which gives further reason to identify Hiruko with Ebisu. It is said that Ebisu is the only god who does not attend the assembly of all the gods held at the Izumo Shrine in October.

In considering Hiruko's fate, it is worthwhile mentioning that the merchants constituted the lowest class in the feudal age, behind the highest class of the warriors followed by the farmers and the artisans. In this sense, Ebisu had been regarded as a "low class" god. It is natural to imagine that the discarded god returned to the shores of Japan and stayed there secretly as a god in a low class. However, recently in Japan the popularity of Ebisu has increased greatly, reflecting the fact that people's attitude towards business has completely changed. The class structure of contemporary Japan, as reflected in the minds of its people, constitutes a complete reversal of the feudal structure. Today, business is most highly regarded, followed by manufacturing, agriculture, and the army at the bottom. My fear is that Hiruko has moved into the center of the Japanese pantheon as the god of business. Some Japanese today go abroad expressing the male sun aspect in connection with business but not much in other fields. Hiruko is needed today, but it is nonsense to limit his function to the field of business. In order to prevent the invasion of Ebisu into the center of the Japanese pantheon, the Japanese must use their imagination and find a fitting place for the male sun.

10. The Fate of Katako

At this point, I would like to tell you a Japanese fairy tale which may shed some light on Hiruko's fate. It is a variation on "The Laughter of Oni."[1] It is a parallel to the myth of the Sun Goddess' retreat into the cave. The story I would like to examine here is entitled "Katako," which means "Half-child," and briefly runs as follows:

1. Hayao Kawai, "The Laughter of Oni," *Spring* 1985, Dallas, TX.

Once upon a time, there was a certain couple, and one day the husband meets an oni (a kind of devil). The oni asks him whether he likes rice cakes. He answers jokingly that he likes them so much he would trade his wife for some. The oni gives him a lot of rice cakes, which the man happily eats. When he goes home, however, he realizes that the oni has taken his word seriously, for his wife has disappeared. The man sets out to find his wife and travels around in vain for ten years. He finally realizes that he has to go to the island of the oni. Upon arriving by boat, he meets a boy about ten years old who is half-human and half-oni. The boy explains that his name was Katako (Half-child) because his father is the chief of the onis and his mother is Japanese. (It is interesting to note that Katako says that his mother is Japanese instead of a human being.) The boy says that his mother longs to go back to Japan and gazes at the sea everyday.

Katako takes the man to his home where the man meets Katako's mother. She turns out to be the man's wife. The couple wants to return to Japan but the oni will not allow it. The oni proposes a contest, which, if the man wins, would allow the couple to go back home. Whenever the man has difficulty, Katako helps him to win. With that help from Katako, the couple is able to go back to Japan, and they take him with them.

The story does not end yet, and goes on to tell us some incredible things.

Katako stays in Japan with the couple but everybody calls him "Oniko" (Child of Oni) and does not befriend him at all. Katako feels it very difficult to stay there and says to his mother, "If I die, cut the oni part of my body into pieces, spit them out and leave them in front of the door. Then no oni will be able to enter the house. If any oni dares to try, throw stones at his eyes." After that he climbs a tall tree and falls to his death. The mother cries, but does what Katako had asked her to do. One day the oni comes to the couple's house. He cannot enter so he shouts, "Japanese women are horrible!

They spit out their own children's flesh!" The oni tries to break in but the couple prevent him by throwing stones at his eyes.

I would like to focus on Katako's suicide. Katako, who was so helpful in bringing his mother back to Japan, has to commit suicide because he has difficulty in relating to the Japanese. Because the story is tragic, I tried to find other variations which could give us some clues about how to rescue Katako from his difficulty. I could not find any. However, one version tells us that Katako goes back to his father's land because of the difficulty of staying in Japan. In another, when Katako grows up, he cannot help eating human beings. So he asks his grandfather to kill him; otherwise he would continue to eat men. The grandfather answers that he could never kill his own grandson even though he is the child of an oni. Then Katako says, "It can't be helped. I will kill myself." He goes to the mountains and builds a hut in the woods. He enters it and sets it on fire. After he dies in the fire, the ashes become mosquitos and leeches, which, as we know, suck human blood.

This is a truly horrible ending. The transformation of Katako's ashes into leeches makes us realize, however, the secret relation between Katako and Hiruko. It dawned on me that the oni in this story might be the offspring of the Leech Child, the carrier of strong masculinity. I fantasized that the Leech Child drifted to an island after he was expelled from Japan. He found a woman there who could accept his masculinity. The offspring of this Leech Child became onis because they not only inherited his strong masculinity but also his resentment toward the Japanese, who could not accept him. Katako, who is burdened by both of these insofar as he is half-oni, could not live in Japan very long. No one asked him to go back to his father's land. Nobody harmed him. And yet he could not relate to the Japanese. This unseen pressure finally forced him to commit suicide. The oni's statement, "Japanese women are horrible (because) they spit out their own children's flesh," is quite revealing. It shows that the femininity of the Japanese has a very cruel aspect; it rejects its own flesh and blood in order to protect itself from being invaded by strong masculinity.

It is also worth reflecting on the fact that Katako asks his grandfather to kill him. This is reminiscent of one of Grimm's fairy tales, "The Golden Bird." In it, the hero is helped in various ways by a fox. At the end of the story, when everything seems to be happily concluded, the fox asks the hero to kill it. The hero is naturally quite reluctant to do so, but finally agrees because the fox entreats him so passionately. When the fox is killed and dismembered, it is reborn as a splendid prince. What would have happened if the Japanese grandfather had killed Katako in accordance with the latter's wishes? I do not think that a sudden transformation would have taken place as it did with the fox in Grimm's story because Katako was half-Japanese. The only path open to him was to commit suicide. His rebirth as a leech suggests that he could only make the Japanese remember him by sucking their blood.

When I see Katako's story in this light, I realize that there are many Katakos living amongst the Japanese today. I do not want them to commit suicide or go back to their father's land. Nor do I feel that a quick transformation can be effected by killing them. The only path left is to keep them alive in Japan however difficult it may be. Our constant efforts to do so may cause some changes in the Japanese people. I have no idea what these changes might be, but I am certain that we have to keep these Katakos alive even though it is an enormously difficult task.

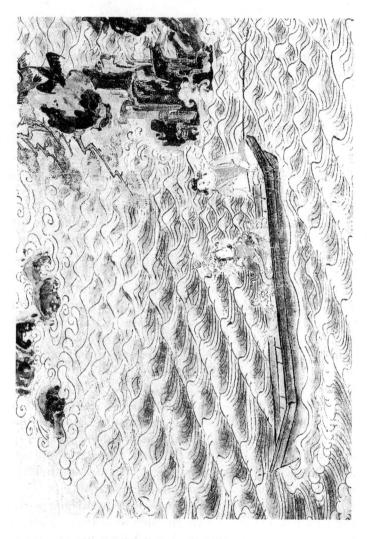

Figure 9. Urashima and the Turtle Princess

IV. Japanese Fairy Tales:
The Aesthetic Solution

1. The Tale of Urashima

The word *beauty* may be rendered in Japanese as *ut-sukushi, uruwashi,* or *yoshi.* The last word, *yoshi, is* especially interesting because it can mean, "good," "able," and "well." In Japan, especially in ancient times, aesthetic value and ethical value were inseparable. Beauty is probably the most important element in understanding Japanese culture. In fairy tales too, beauty plays a great role in the construction of the stories.

I would like to begin with a story called *Urashima-taro,* a tale which is quite popular in Japan. The story is found all over Japan in many versions, some going back to the 8th Century. The story has of course changed, and its present form is contained in the following summary:

> Once upon a time there lived a young man called Urashi-motaro. One day he rescued a turtle which had been caught by children. A few days later, the turtle took Urashima to the Dragon palace at the bottom of the sea in order to repay his kindness. Urashima was moved by the beauty of the palace. The princess Otohime welcomed him with her beautiful maids. Urashima was very happy to stay there for three days. When he wished to return, the princess gave him a casket, saying that he should not open it under any circumstances. When he returned home he was astonished to find that three hundred years had passed since he had left. Completely desperate, he opened the casket in spite of the princess' prohibition, whereupon white smoke came out of the box, and Urashima became an old man.

Every Japanese today knows this tale. One who is familiar with fairy tales in Europe may have an odd feeling about this story: it has no happy ending, nor any story about a marriage even though a young man meets a beautiful lady. In fact, Urashima does marry the princess in an early version of the story, which is recorded in the *Tango-fudoki*[1] written at the beginning of the 8th Century. In the *Tango-fudoki* version, Urashima has been fishing on the sea for three days and three nights without catching any fish. Finally he catches a five-colored turtle. The turtle turns into a lady whose beauty is beyond comparison. She proposes to Urashima, and he accepts immediately. Later on she takes him to a palace at the bottom of the sea. The remainder of the story is almost identical to the one cited here.

In the *Tango-fudoki* version, Urashima marries the princess. However, it is worth noting that the woman proposes first to the man and that their marriage is not at all a happy one. It is also interesting to note that the old version contains no motive for repaying kindness.

2. The Dragon Fight

The following episode reveals a typical Western reaction to the tale of Urashima. A Russian ethnologist, Chistov, once told Urashima's story to his four-year-old grandson.[2] While Chistov was reading a rather long description of the beauty of the Dragon Palace, he noticed that the boy showed no interest and in fact seemed to expect something different. He asked his grandson what he was

1. Tango-Fudoki, in *Fudoki* (in Japanese), Iwanamishoten 1958.
2. K. Chistov, "Why Russian Readers Can Understand Japanese Fairy Tales" in T. Ozawa, ed., *Nipponjin to Minwa* (Japanese and Fairy Tales) (in Japanese), Gyoosei 1976.

thinking. The boy told him that he had been expecting the hero to fight with a dragon in the palace. The boy could not understand why the hero did not fight with a dragon and did not marry the princess.

Hearing the name Dragon Palace, Westerners tend to associate it with a dragon fight, whereas Japanese associate it with the beauty of the palace. One of the versions which describes its beauty runs as follows:

> When Urashima opened the window to the east, it seemed to be springtime. The whole place was alive with blossoms of cherries and plums. The willows were flowing in the wind. Birds flew out of the mist and sang songs in front of the house. The tops of the trees were full of blossoms. When he looked to the south, it was summer. Beside the fence which divided the garden into spring and summer, Japanese sunflowers were in full bloom. Lotus flowers were in a pond....

I will not continue the story here as I am afraid that you might be bored, like the Russian boy, by a long description of the scenery, of autumn in the west and of winter in the north. You can imagine how tired the four-year-old boy was of hearing about flowers, birds, mist, dew and snow instead of being told of a courageous fight with a dragon! One may wonder where a dragon ought to be as nothing is said about it other than the fact that the palace was called the Dragon Palace. I don't know where it ought to be, but I have a feeling that the long descriptions about beautiful Nature in Japanese fairy tales is something equivalent to that of dragon fights in Western fairy tales. In Western stories, the hero kills the dragon and marries a maiden afterwards.[1] The marriage is said to be a symbol of the union of opposites. It is true that marriage does not play a big role in Japanese fairy tales. How-

---

1. About the symbolic meaning of the Dragon Fight, cf. E. Neumann, *Origin and History of Consciousness,* Pantheon Books 1954.

ever, the coexistence of the four seasons at the same time could be a symbol of the union of opposites. One can notice a striking contrast between the use of symbol in the West and in Japan. The Western symbol consists of human beings, whereas the Japanese symbol consists of Nature. Considering what I have just said, the killing of the dragon might signify the destruction of Nature. The heroic establishment of the masculine ego might cause the destruction of Mother Nature. But I have no intention of arguing that the lack of dragon fights in Japanese fairy tales shows their superiority to Western fairy tales.

Even though the coexistence of the four seasons symbolizes the union of opposites, Urashima could bring home only a casket, which caused him to become old. Urashima has many wonderful adventures in the Dragon Palace where the sense of time was experienced differently from that in this world. But his life in his native land afterwards was tragic. Some versions say that he died when he opened the casket. It might be well that he did not fight a dragon. The ending itself was already unhappy enough.

3. Aesthetic Solution to Conflicts

Almost all the tales of Urashima in Japan have unhappy endings involving Urashima's death or aging. A few have different endings. In one of these tales, the princess gives Urashima a casket with three drawers, saying "Please open them if you are completely at a loss." He opens them when he finds that hundreds of years have passed upon his return. In the first drawer, there are a pair of crane wings. White smoke comes from the second one. In the third one he finds a mirror. When he sees himself in this mirror, he notices he has become an old man. Then wings stick to his back, and he becomes a crane. While he is flying around above his mother's tomb, the princess comes to shore and transforms herself into a turtle. The last sentence of the story is: "The Ise folksong, in which it is sung that a crane and a turtle dance together, comes from this story."

Even though some efforts have been made to avoid an unhappy ending, the ending itself may be different from what Westerners expect. To explain this last scene, I should add that the crane and the turtle are symbols of longevity in Japan. One of the most celebrated and favorite scenes in Japan is a turtle on shore and a crane flying above pine-trees nearby. For Japanese people, a scene of natural beauty is more desirable than a happy ending to a story.

Another kind of ending taken from a Japanese myth[1] has some similarities to Urashima's story:

> A young god, named Ho-wori, goes down to the bottom of the sea in order to seek a huck which he has borrowed from his brother and lost in the sea. There he meets a beautiful princess, Toyotama-hime, and they are married. After staying three years, he returns home to give back the huck to his brother. Some days later, Toyotama-hime comes forth from the sea. She tells her husband that she is going to give birth to a child. He orders built a parturition hut thatched with commorant feathers. But before the thatching is completed, she enters the hut feeling birth to be imminent. When she is about to deliver the child, she tells her husband that he should not look into the room, since she is going to revert to her original form while giving birth. Thinking her words strange, he watches her in secret as she is about to give birth. He is astonished to see that his wife turns into a giant crocodile, and he flees in fright. Toyotama-hime is ashamed when

1. *Kojiki,* translated with an Introduction and Notes by D.L. Philippi, Princeton University Press 1968.

she discovers that her husband has seen her original form. She departs, leaving behind the baby she has borne.

Toyotama-hime cannot subdue her wish to see her husband again although she resents him for having looked at her. She therefore sends her younger sister back to the birthplace to nurse the child, entrusting her with the following song:

> Beautiful are red jewels
> Even their cord seems to sparkle.
> But I prefer white jewels
> For the awesome beauty
> Of white jewels like form.

Then Ho-wori replies with the song:

> As long as I have life
> I shall never forget
> My beloved, with whom I slept
> On an island where wild ducks,
> Birds of the offing, came to land.

There is a strong conflict in the heroine's mind. She is bitter at him for having transgressed her prohibition, yet at the same time her yearning for her husband is strong. As a solution to this conflict, she writes a poem. The exchange of songs tells us the end of the story. Actually, in some versions of Urashima, we find exchanges of songs between the man and the woman at the end of the stories.

James Hillman, while staying in Japan, once remarked that the Japanese like "aesthetic solutions to conflicts." The ending to the story of Urashima is a beautiful image, and the myth with the exchange of songs is a fine example of this sort of resolution. It is remarkable that the goddess neither becomes angry nor metes out any punishment to the transgressor, who sees her naked, original form. It is worth comparing this tale with the story of

Artemis and Aktaion in Greek mythology. There the goddess becomes so angry with Aktaion that she turns him
into a deer, which is finally killed by his own dogs. Contrary to this, the Japanese goddess is not stirred to anger,
but instead just disappears. The exchange of the poems
forms a solution to the conflict.

4. The Forbidden Chamber

Another Japanese fairy tale called "The Bush Warblers'
Home"[1] is as follows:

A young woodcutter goes into a forest, where he finds a
splendid house that he had neither seen nor heard of before. Entering the house, he meets a beautiful lady who asks
him to stay there while she briefly goes away. As she is leaving, she forbids him to look into the next room. He promises not to do so. Once he is alone, however, he breaks the
promise and enters the next room. Three beautiful girls are
sweeping the room, but upon seeing the woodcutter, they
immediately disappear, gliding away quickly like birds. The
woodcutter then goes into one room after another in the
house, seeing that they contain many treasures. In the sev-
enth room there is a bird-nest with three small eggs. Picking
them up, he accidentally drops them. Three birds come out
of the eggs and fly away. Just then the lady returns, blaming
the woodcutter for breaking his promise and thereby causing the death of her three daughters. Transforming herself
into a bush warbler, she too flies away. When the man comes
to his senses again, he finds himself standing alone in the
same place where he had found the house: but the house is
no longer there.

1. Japanese fairy tales are recorded and classified in the following
work: K. Seki, ed. *Nippon Mukashibanashi Taisei* (Collection of Japanese
Fairy Tales) (in Japanese), Kadokawa Shoten 1978-80, Vols. 1-12. Here
"Bush Warblers' Home" is classified as No. 196 A. with many variants.

You may have noticed some similarities between this story and the myth told before. When the men break their promises, the heroines do not punish them; they just leave. The stories do not tell much about the feelings of the women. But I sense a deep feeling of sorrow for both of the women.

If we compare this story with the Western fairy tale of Bluebeard, the difference is quite obvious. In Bluebeard the prohibitor is a male and the transgressor a female. When the heroine enters the forbidden chamber, her husband simply tries to kill her. There is also a remarkable difference concerning what the transgressors see in the forbidden chambers. The Japanese see many treasures, whereas in the Western fairy tales they see the most awful scenes of corpses.

In order to know the characteristics of the forbidden chambers, I have studied about twenty different versions of the story, gathered from all over Japan. The most frequent feature in the forbidden rooms is "A bush warbler with plum blossoms." The scene is one of the most celebrated in Japan, just like a scene involving a turtle and a crane with pine-trees.

The hero also often sees a series of images which reflect the four changing seasons. Some heroes see four scenes which reflect the stages of the growth of rice. In another variant, there are four rooms, one of which is the forbidden chamber. In the other three rooms the man sees summer, autumn and winter. In the last room he sees spring, namely, a bush warbler with plum blossoms.

Before making a comparison between the forbidden chamber motif in Japan and that in the West, I would like to present the dreams of two Japanese. In both, the beauty of Nature is of great significance.

5. Dreams of the Japanese

I once analyzed a male university student who was very bright and had studied in the United States for a year. After a period of analysis, he dreamed of his mother's death. The next day he dreamed that, with the help of the two persons, he tried to assassinate a feudal lord who looked like his father. He added in his associations that one of these two persons looked like his analyst. Two weeks later he brought me the following dream:

> He noticed that he had three legs. Then he had a strong urge to see a cross. The cross should have been attached to a pine-tree. He secretly entered a Buddhist temple where the pine-tree was supposed to be. He went into a dark room where several men and women were lying. He could not recognize the men. But one of the women was beautiful. She had an exotic face with heavy make-up. For an instant he felt an urge to rape her.
>
> There was another woman from whom he asked directions to the pine-tree. She pointed into the next room. Upon opening the door he found several ill persons lying there. The room was filled with the odor of medicine. Passing through the room, he went into a corridor where he saw a garden. It was covered by lawn, and a pine-tree was there. The sun light was dazzlingly white. He could not find the cross, but he did notice a bush warbler on a plum-tree. The bird was cheerfully sipping nectar from the blossoms and was innocently enjoying life. This was really heaven, he thought. He was very pleased and thought, how good it was that he had come here.

Before having this dream, the analysand dreamed of his mother's death and his intention to kill a person like his father. As I noted, he had been influenced strongly by Western culture. I had expected that his anima figure would appear in his dreams in due course. So I was deeply impressed with this dream with a bush warbler on a plum-tree. The analysand himself was very surprised to have this kind of dream with such time-honored Japanese symbols.

In the dream, he has three legs, which suggests an unusual power received after his parents' death. Obviously he is annoyed with the three legs and wants to be returned to normal. Hence he feels a strong urge to see a cross, for him a Christian symbol. But in the dream he is convinced that the cross is attached to a pine-tree in a Buddhist temple. A pine-tree, as I mentioned before, is greatly honored in Japan and symbolizes longevity. A cross at a pine-tree in a Buddhist temple is a rather strange mixture of symbols from the West and the East. In the dream he enters a temple where he meets a beautiful woman. The exotic face suggests that she might be a Westerner. He feels an urge to be united with her. But it is too violent and vanishes in a moment. Afterwards he sees a typical Japanese scene instead of the cross which he wants to see. He is deeply impressed by the scene, and his words, "How good it was that I came here!" suggest that he feels good that he has come into analysis.

Next, I would like to relate the case of a female university student. She came to see me because she had been annoyed by hallucinatory voices, which told her indecent things. She was raised by a strict mother who hated to speak about sex. So far she had no boyfriend because, in her home, falling in love was supposed to be vulgar. The indecent voices came from her shadow side which was expected to be integrated to her one-sided ego. After a period of analysis, she brought the following dream which had made a deep impression on her:

> She found two precious boxes made of paulownia wood. Opening them, she found that one contained four pieces of

precious paper of red color and that the other contained four pieces of precious paper of white color. On the four papers, poems about the four seasons were written. She read:

In Spring...
In Summer...
In Autumn...
In Winter....

When she awoke, she forgot the rest of the poems. On awaking, she felt for the first time the possibility of being allowed to love a member of the opposite sex. She said, "Love does exist in this world, just as the four seasons exist in this world." She added in her associations that red meant passion to her and that white meant purity. In her dream, the red and white papers on which the poems of the four seasons were written suggest a possibility of the integration of her shadow side.

6. The West and the East

So far I have indicated that the beauty of Nature is important in Japanese fairy tales and dreams. In order to make its importance more distinct, I would like to compare the Japanese Bush Warblers' Home tales with those Western fairy tales which have the motif of the forbidden chamber. In addition to the Bluebeard story, cited earlier, I would like to relate a story called "The Three Eyes"[1] from Cyprus. In that story, a girl marries a stranger who is quite rich. He hands her a hundred and one keys to the rooms in his house. He says to her that she may use any of them except the last one. As we might expect, she opens

1. F. Karlinger, *Inselmärchen des Mittelmeeres,* Eugen Diederichs Verlag 1960.

the forbidden chamber only to find that her husband has transformed himself into a monster with three eyes and is eating corpses. The scene is more horrible than anything to be found in the Bluebeard tales. The Three Eyes tries to kill her, but a king rescues her by killing the monster. Marriage is the happy ending.

If we compare this story with that of the Bush Warblers' Home, the contrasts are remarkable in every detail. In the Cypriot story, the prohibitor and the transgressor are male and female respectively, whereas in Japanese fairy tales, they are reversed. In the forbidden chambers, we see the brutal scene with corpses, while in the other we see the beauty of Nature. Death is a suitable punishment for the transgressor in the West, whereas no punishment is given in Japan. Finally the outcomes of the stories are completely different; the heroine in the West is rescued by a splendid man and marries him, whereas the heroine of the Japanese tale leaves the man alone and vanishes.

Here I would like to note an interesting detail found in the Bluebeard tale, where the heroine asks her sister what she can see in the field while Bluebeard is waiting to kill his wife. Her sister answers, "I cannot see anything but the shining sun and green herbs." It is very important to notice that the description of Nature – the shining sun and green herbs – means nothing to the heroine. What she expects to see are human beings, her brothers, not the beauty of Nature.

7. Beauty and Ugliness

The Japanese legend called *Adachigahara* ("the field of Adachi") is a horrible story. A Buddhist monk on a journey arrives at the field of Adachi at night. He begs a lady living there alone for lodging. She grants his request. Before she goes to get firewood, she asks him not to look into her bedroom. The monk, however, cannot subdue his curiosity. He opens the door to her bedroom and is utterly astonished to see the room full of decayed corpses. He runs away. As soon as the lady notices this, she transforms herself into Oni, a Japanese demon, and chases him. The monk recites a Buddhist sutra, which causes Oni to leave and disappear.

In this legend, the inside of the forbidden chamber is just like the hidden chamber in the Bluebeard and the Three Eyes tales. The big difference is that in Japan the prohibitor is a female and the transgressor is male whereas in the West they are reversed.

As far as the contents of the forbidden chamber are concerned, it is striking to note the contrast between that of the legend of *Adachigahara* and that of the fairy tale of the Bush Warblers' Home. How can the difference be explained? In order to clarify this problem, I will discuss another story myth, in which a god transgresses a goddess' prohibition:

> Izanagi and Izanami are the first parents in Japanese myth.[1] The goddess Izanami gives birth to everything in the world. Finally, by giving birth to fire, she is burned and dies. Her husband, Izanagi, laments and visits the underworld to find his dead wife. The goddess Izanami says to her husband that it would be difficult for her to go back as she has already eaten something from the underworld, but she will discuss the problem with gods of the underworld. Then she asks him to wait for a while and not to look at her until she comes back. It is completely dark, so he can see nothing. However, the god cannot wait any longer and makes a fire. He sees his wife in a terrible state of disintegration; maggots are squirming and roaring on the corpse. Hereupon he is awestruck and flees. The goddess says, "He has shamed me!" and pur-

1. Kojiki, *ibid.*

sues him with the hags of the underworld. Through a magic flight he succeeds in returning to this world. He moves a tremendous rock and closes the pass between this world and the underworld. The god and the goddess stand facing each other, one on each side of the rock. She tells him she will cause the death of one thousand people each day in this world. Whereupon the god replies that he will build one thousand and five hundred parturition huts each day.

In Japanese mythology, one can find many important compromises instead of fights between counterparts. The compromise between Izanami and Izanagi is really the first one made between a male and a female, or between this world and the underworld. However, as can be seen, the solution to conflict is not at all aesthetic.

If we recall the Ho-wori and Toyotama-hime story in which the betrayed goddess sends songs to her husband, we can see that this is also a kind of compromise between a male and a female, or between this world and the world beneath the sea. It becomes aesthetic since they exchange songs instead of arguing about how many persons will be killed.

8. Transgression and Consciousness

In all these Japanese stories, the prohibitors are always females, and the transgressors are always males. In considering this problem, I would like to point out that the transgressions are related to the elevation of consciousness.

After Izanagi transgresses his wife's prohibition, he runs away and closes the pass between this world and the underworld with a gigantic rock. This means that he makes a separation between the two worlds. The same thing can be said in the myth of Ho-wori and Toyotama-hime: When the god breaks his promise to his wife, the goddess goes back to the palace under the sea and never returns. This world and the world beneath the sea have been separated since. Separation has to do with consciousness. Consciousness wants to make distinctions, without which everything is in chaos. These myths are, therefore, really myths of consciousness.

As we know, the same theme exists in the Old Testament: Adam and Eve transgress God's prohibition. After the transgression, the land of God and the land of human beings are separated. This is the story of paradise lost but at the same time it is the one of the elevation of consciousness in human beings.

The differences between the Japanese myths and those of the Christian tradition may be summarized as follows: 1) The sexes of the transgressors and the prohibitors are reversed between them. 2) In the West the transgression is made by human beings against God, but in Japan it is made among gods. 3) God in the West metes out strong punishment, whereas the Japanese goddess does not.

The first point suggests the predominance of the male principle in the West and of the female principle in Japan. In the West, God in Heaven is the prohibitor, whereas in Japan, it is the goddess of the great Mother. Neither God in the West nor the goddess in Japan want human beings to have their consciousness. They prohibit human beings from knowing something. Yet, in spite of the gods' suppression, human beings must have their consciousness. They break the prohibitions imposed by the gods. Western consciousness is established at the cost of great punishment. But what of the Japanese stories? Why is there no punishment in Japan? One of the reasons for this is that the events occur between gods, not between God and human beings. I think it is appropriate that the gods and goddesses make a compromise instead of one punishing the other.

Moreover, in the Izanagi and Izanami story, the great goddess dies giving birth to fire. In mythology, the elevation of consciousness is related to the myth of making or stealing fire. Fire can be a symbol of consciousness. The various mythologies of the world tell us how difficult it is for humankind to make fire. In Japanese mythology, human beings do not have to make any particular effort to obtain fire as the great goddess gives birth to fire at the cost of her own life. Human beings simply accept it. What an easy task it is! I am afraid, however, that the Japanese accept not only fire but also the death of the goddess who pays for it.

The generosity of the great goddess continues so as not to give much punishment to the god who breaks his promise. As I mentioned earlier, the goddess Toyotama-hime does not assign any punishment to Ho-wori when he sees her in her original form as a crocodile. In Japanese mythology, the goddesses' shame is more stressed than the sins of the transgressors. The great goddess says, "He has shamed me!" when her husband sees her dead body. Toyotama-hime also "felt extremely ashamed" when her crocodile form is seen by her husband in spite of her prohibition. (In Japan, goddesses are so ashamed that there is no room for human beings to commit the original sin!)

The consciousness of the Japanese is thus established without original sin. It is necessary, however (as the myth reveals), that the gods must see the terrible side of the female whose principle is dominant in their culture. This corresponds to the fact that, in Western fairy tales, heroines must see the terrible side of the male whose principle prevails in their culture.

9. Legends and Fairy Tales

What, then, of the beautiful scenes seen by Japanese heroes in fairy tales? In order to explain why men in Japanese fairy tales see the beauty of Nature, I would like to return to the Japanese legend, *Adachigahara*. Inasmuch as the monk in this legend sees corpses in the forbidden chamber, the legend is in line with the myth. In the ending of the legend, however, one finds Buddhist influence. The Oni (the demon) disappears as the monk chants a Buddhist sutra. The problem is why such a difference between the legend and the fairy tale exists? In the fairy tale, the male no longer sees the dark side of the female, but sees instead the beauty of Nature.

It is difficult to make general comments about the difference between fairy tales and legends. Max Lüthi[1] indicates that features in fairy tales are more elaborated than those in legends. It may also be that in legends the stories are tragic and heroes are not rewarded for their good deeds, whereas in fairy tales the hero who does good deeds is always repaid, and there is a happy ending. It is interesting that even in the West one can find legends which have tragic endings. In some German legends, for example, water nymphs, who are transformed into and marry human beings, leave their families immediately when their origins are revealed. This results in unhappy endings like those in Japanese fairy tales. As far as legends are concerned, then, one is struck by the similarity between Japan and the West.

Fairy tales are more elaborated than legends. My conclusion is that Westerners tend to elaborate fairy tales with ethical intentions whereas the Japanese elaborate them with aesthetic ones. In the West, the hero's virtue is

1. M. Lüthi, *Es war einmal – Vom Wesen des Volksmärchens*, Vandenhoeck und Ruprecht 1962.

rewarded by a happy ending. But in Japan, beautiful endings are much preferred to happy endings. In the story of
the Bush Warblers' Home, for example, Japanese at least
feel that the ending is beautiful.

In Japan there are many fairy tales in which animals or
plants become transformed into beautiful women and
marry young men. However, the results are almost always
unhappy. The following fairy tale, entitled "A Flower-
Wife,"[1] seems to be typically Japanese, though it is not
popular there:

> There lived a young pack-horse man in a village. Every
> morning he went to a mountain to gather grass for his horse.
> While cutting grass, he sang songs in a beautiful voice. One
> evening a pretty woman visited him and asked him for lodg-
> ing for the night. He declined her request as he could not
> cook well. But she said she could do very well for both of
> them. Indeed, she managed quite well, and she proposed
> marriage to him. They married and lived happily. One
> morning, after coming home from a mountain, the young
> husband wanted to show his wife a beautiful evening prim-
> rose which he had cut with the grass. But he was astonished
> to find that his wife had collapsed in the kitchen: She told
> him that she was the spirit of the very evening primrose he
> had cut that morning. She had been attracted by his beauti-
> ful voice and had transformed herself into a human being in
> order to marry him. Then she said, "Now my life is ending.
> Thank you very much for everything." And she died.

This is a tragic story. But it is beautiful. Moreover,
there is no evil being in it. The young man, the woman,
the evening primrose – everything is beautiful. The man
cuts the primrose with good intentions, wanting to show
it to his beloved wife. Nevertheless, the ending is tragic.

In Grimm's fairy tales, there are three stories in which
girls were changed into flowers.[2] In all these stories, the

1. K. Seki, *ibid.*, New Type No. 8.
2. *Grimm's Fairy Tales*, Nos. 56, 78, 160.

flowers become human beings again and marry happily in the end. In one story, "The Stones,"[1] a flower becomes human again when a man breaks its stalk. This shows a striking contrast with the Japanese story, in which the flower-wife meets her death when the flower's stalk is cut by the man. In the Grimm's tale, the flowers are originally human beings who change by some magical powers. Human beings, especially men, must accomplish something to overcome the magic spell. In the Japanese story, it is originally a plant which becomes transformed into a human being. It is worth noticing that nothing is mentioned about any magic in this transformation. It is taken for granted. The demarcation between plants and human beings is quite thin. In this sense the story of the Flower-Wife is at the same time one of both plants and human beings.

The evening primrose is beautiful. Its beauty attracts the man so much that he cuts the flower to show it to his beloved wife, bringing about her death. The flower is especially beautiful because death exists behind it. Or one can say that a flower is beautiful only when it can bring the deep feeling of sorrow. The stories of the Bush Warbler's Home and the Flower-Wife both show the beauty of Nature. But the meaning of these stories is completed only when we take into account the feelings of the listeners. They must be shocked by the tragic endings and feel very sad. That feeling is necessary for the completion of the story about beauty. Beauty is complete only when sorrowful feeling accompanies it.

The evening primrose itself is beautiful, but still its beauty is not complete. It becomes complete only when its death is brought on. Or, one can say, if we see not only the flower of the evening primrose, but also the death

1. *Ibid*, No. 160.

which it inevitably contains, we can appreciate its beauty of completeness. The story of the Bush Warbler's Home also contains the motive of death. The story is obviously one of spring. It is the season of the birth of life. The story tells us, however, that the beauty of spring is complete only insofar as one foresees its death; in the end of the story we are told that the maiden, symbolizing the beauty of spring, just disappears.

In the Grimm's story, a flower changes into a beautiful girl when a man breaks its stalk. This means death to the flower. Here might be hidden an idea similar to what we have seen earlier in Japanese fairy tales. Behind the beautiful girl one can see the death of the flower. However, one forgets about death quickly in this story because it is followed by a rebirth of the flower into a human being. The story is then completed through the union of man and woman.

10. The Beauty of Perfection and Completeness

Jung points out the distinction between perfection and completeness in the ethical dimension. He is concerned, as we know, with the problem of evil. How can we explain the existence of evil in this world? In his attempt to cope with the problem he arrives at the ideas of perfection and completeness, combining them with the distinction between masculine and feminine principles.

> Perfection is a masculine desideratum, while a woman inclines by nature to completeness. And it is a fact that even today, a man can stand a relative state of perfection much better and for a longer period than a woman, while as a rule it does not agree with women and may even be dangerous for them. If a woman strives for perfection she forgets the complementary role of completeness, which, though imperfect

by itself, forms the necessary counterpart to perfection. For, just as completeness is always imperfect, so perfection is always incomplete, and therefore represents a final state which is hopelessly sterile. "Ex perfecto nihil fit," say the old masters, whereas the imperfectum carries within it the seeds of its own improvement. Perfectionism always ends in a blind alley, while completeness by itself lacks selective values.[1]

Noticeably, Jung does not value one over the other: "Completeness is always imperfect, so perfection is always incomplete."

Beautiful women appear in both the fairy tales of the West and of Japan. In Western stories, the fact that heroes finally succeed in getting women suggests that completeness occurs in the ethical dimension, whereas in the Japanese fairy tales, the fact that beautiful women just vanish or die, leaving a deep feeling of sorrow, symbolizes completeness in the aesthetic dimension. It is the beauty of completeness.

It is difficult to make a general comment about whether Japanese like the beauty of perfection or the beauty of completeness. It is not very easy to make comments on what is orthodox and what is a compensation. As Jung says, completeness by itself lacks selective values. It is difficult to say what is orthodox in Japan because Japanese values are based on the principle of completeness rather than of perfection. It is true that there is a strong tendency for Japanese to underestimate the beauty of perfection. There is a famous saying that men should not appreciate the cherry only in its full blossom and the moon only in its full light. "No path leads beyond perfection into the future – there is only a turning back, a collapse of the ideal," says Jung.[2] Because of this attitude in Japanese,

1. C.G. Jung, "Answer to Job," in *Collected Works of C.G. Jung*, Vol. 11, 1958, p. 395.
2. *Answer to Job*, p. 399.

it is said that Japanese like imperfect beauty, or that they think the state of imperfection is more beautiful than the state of perfection. I think it is much better to say that there is a tendency in the Japanese to appreciate the beauty of completeness.

In order to show why I prefer the phrase "the beauty of completeness" to "the imperfect beauty," I will present you an example. There is a famous story about a Zen master who shows what beauty is for him. A young monk is sweeping a garden. He tries to do his best at the job. He cleans the garden perfectly so that no dust is left in it. Contrary to his expectation the old master is not happy about his work. The young monk thinks for a while and shakes a tree so that several dead leaves fall down here and there in the garden. The master smiles when he sees that.

I would like to call this the beauty of completeness. When the young man tries to sweep the garden in order not to leave any dust, he is striving for the beauty of perfection. The garden with some dead leaves is the beauty of completeness. It is better not to call it imperfect beauty. The beauty of perfection is achieved by renouncing everything that is ugly, whereas the beauty of completeness contains things which are not necessarily beautiful.

Let us return to the myth in which the goddess Izanami forbids her husband Izanagi to see her dead body. The fact that the prohibitors are always women in Japanese tales reflects the predominance of the feminine principle in Japan. That the god saw the terrible state of the goddess shows the necessity of knowing the dark side of the feminine. It corresponds to the fact that women come to know the dark side of men in Western fairy tales. After seeing the dark side of the feminine, the male and the female make a compromise in the Japanese myth. At this point there occurs an important event. The god

Izanagi purifies himself in a river. It is a purification ceremony. I mentioned earlier that it is difficult to make a
general comment about what is orthodox in Japan. Yet
one can say that purity is very important. The purification
of defilement carries much more weight than the redemption of sins. I even doubt whether such a concept as
the redemption of sins exists in ancient Japan. In this
sense the perfect purity is the ideal for which Japanese
strive. This is what the myth of the purification ceremony
tells us. The fairy tales show an interesting compensation
for it. The myth tells us that the male god experiences a
perfect purification after he sees the defilement of the
corpses. The fairy tales, however, also tell us that the forbidden chamber does not contain anything defiled. One
can find there the beauty of completeness, but not the
beauty of perfection. In the forbidden chambers death is
no longer associated with defilement. It is a part of the
beauty of completeness. The Japanese fairy tales tell us
that the world is beautiful and that beauty is completed
only if we accept the existence of death.

Figure 10. A young noble man visiting his lover

V. Torikaebaya:

A Tale of Changing Sexual Roles

1. The story of Torikaebaya

Torikaebaya is a story from about the twelfth century. (See the Appendix to this paper for a summary of the story.) The exact date of publication and authorship remain unclear, and scholars continue to debate whether the author is a male or female. One scholar confidently states that only a male could have written the story, while another points to certain passages which he says could only have been written by a woman. One sees it as a comedy, while another regards it as serious fiction.

The story revolves around the motif of sex-role reversal in which a woman marries a woman, and a man tries to make love to a man. I do not know how the people of the time reacted to it, but a prominent modern scholar of Japanese literature found that, "It is unbearable to read." The story has not been seriously considered since, but I myself find it quite interesting and helpful in attempting to understand the psyche.

No personal names appear in the story, making it quite difficult to distinguish the characters. I shall refer to the hero and heroine as "Brother" and "Sister." Pay careful attention to their exchange of roles throughout.

2. The Exchange of Male and Female Roles

This is a peculiar tale, and I can not find any similar stories in Japan or in the literatures of other cultures.

There are stories in which a man disguises himself as a woman and vice versa, but in all of these, as far as I know, the disguise or switch in sex roles is deliberately made for some ulterior motive. The disguised personality takes advantage of others who are tricked by him or her. *Torikaebaya* differs in that the main characters do not change their sex roles deliberately. The plot unfolds independent of their intentions whereas the individual role of the disguised personality forms the central axis of the other stories.

I find some similarity between the heroes of *Torikaebaya* and Iphis and Ianthe in Ovid's *Metamorphoses*. Iphis is a girl but raised as a boy from birth by her mother because her father did not want to have a girl. When Iphis turns thirteen her father has her engaged to a beautiful girl, Ianthe. They fall deeply in love with each other, but Iphis is forlorn as she is well aware that she can not really marry Ianthe. Her mother prays to the goddess Isis that her daughter be transformed into a man. Her wish is fulfilled; Iphis and Ianthe are happily married. In this story the girl Iphis is intentionally raised as a boy. She suffers greatly when the time comes for her to marry. The suffering of the heroine is similar to that of the Sister in *Torikaebaya*. But in Ovid's story the heroine's conflict is solved by the goddess Isis who transforms her into a man, whereas in the Japanese story there is no miracle, and the heroine finds her happiness in truly becoming a woman.

The exchange of sex roles in *Torikaebaya* serves to highlight many essential aspects of the role each sex normally plays. Sister marries a woman and is forced to play the role of a man, but she experiences soft and gentle feelings for the other without sexual relations. She must wait to know her real womanhood until she experiences a man, Chûjô, rather unexpectedly and somewhat violently. She does not stay with Chûjô for long, however, since she can observe him quite objectively with her training as a man. While Chûjô is infatuated with Sister, the latter is able to see from her experience that he is unreliable. Armed with the capacity for objective assessment, she is able to manage the difficult situation with the Emperor and succeed in her role as Empress.

The case of Brother is similar. While Brother acts with confidence once he becomes a real man, the tenderness he experienced as a female helps him to understand women. Sister and Brother combined might form a kind of ideal personality able to act as a man or a woman as the circumstances require.

Their unusual natures are reflected in the fact that Sister becomes Empress and Brother marries a woman of mixed descent, the daughter of a Japanese prince and a Chinese noble. But no supernatural power intervenes, no deity appears as is the case in Ovid's *Metamorphoses*. The combined existence of Sister and Brother is the chemistry that propels the development of the story from beginning to end.

The fantasy of Sister and Brother combining to form a single personality calls to mind Honoré de Balzac's *Séraphita,* a sophisticated work based on the thought of the philosopher-mystic Swedenborg. In *Séraphita* this synthesis of male and female is important in that it shows the way for human beings to attain Heaven. Although the union of the male and female is not explicit in *Torikaebaya,* there is a divine quality to the sibling pair. They cannot be united in the literal sense since they are neither lovers nor husband and wife.

The story of *Torikaebaya* shows that a man does not always have to be "manly," nor a woman always "womanly." It is more fulfilling and useful that a man can be womanly and a woman manly according to the circumstances.

3. Love

In this story there are many kinds of love described: between lovers, couples, parents and children, and friends. One scholar has classified these love-relationships into two major categories: ethical love and decadent love. He sees love between lovers categorically as decadent love and censures it in favor of what he calls ethical love. This critique reflects the Japanese ethos as a whole in which love between a man and a woman is generally not given high regard.

I, however, cannot agree with this simplistic classification. I am struck by the fact that each of the different loves, between lovers, husband and wife, parents and children, forms a unique strand in a beautiful tapestry of human lives. In this tale of criss-crossing romance it is remarkable that there is almost no jealousy. This can be attributed to the ingenuity of the author who incorporated some unique features into his story.

Jealousy is first avoided by the fact that Sister and Brother are in a sense bisexual. When Sister realizes that "his" wife is having a love affair with Chûjô, Sister feels self-pity and pity for "his" wife because "he" knows that "he" is not a normal "man." After Sister is acknowledged as a woman, she goes to live with Chûjô in Uji, but the latter often has to visit Sister's former wife. Sister feels somewhat jealous but is able to distance herself from the situation and make an objective assessment due to her experience as a "man." She thus decides to wait until she gives birth to a child, pretending all the while that she loves Chûjô wholeheartedly.

A woman can be like a man and vice versa. By shifting our stance we can avoid unnecessary conflict. If a man and a woman are strongly attached to each other, powerful feelings of jealousy inevitably arise when one learns that the other has been having relations with others. But if they know that each is in a sense bisexual, then the relationship is enriched and there is no room for the crippling power of jealousy to operate.

Secondly, jealousy is avoided through the magnanimity of the Emperor. He does not torment his wife, Sister, when he finds out that she has had a love affair in the past with Chûjô. He does not question her because he senses that a man should know when to stop.

There is only one episode which involves a major conflict caused by love. Here the love-relationship is not that between lovers but between mother and son. When Sister feels the desire to leave Uji, where she has been living with her newborn baby, she experiences the conflict between being a mother and being herself. She wants to leave Chûjô to live her own life but naturally finds it difficult to leave her son behind. Most Japanese women even today would choose to be the mother. Sister, however, chooses a different path:

> Since the bond between parent and child is so deeply rooted, we are sure to cross paths again. No matter how dear my baby may be to me, how can I, once so celebrated by all, go on passing the days in waiting for one man to pay me an occasional visit in this desolate place? (p. 151)

She decides to leave, and the story goes on to relate that, "Sister's strong resolve was rooted in her earlier training as a man." It may seem natural to Western people that she would prefer to be independent rather than rely on a philanderer, but the story was written in the twelfth century, in Japan where the social fabric made such a decision extremely difficult. I also feel that the Western woman who chooses independence often becomes a man to a great extent and sacrifices a great deal of her womanhood.

Sister chooses independence but marries the Emperor. By chance she meets her son in the palace, but she must conceal her real identity and endure her situation. The anguish proves to be overwhelming as tears well up in her eyes, and she says to him, "I am a relative of your mother, and it pains me to see that she yearns for you, seemingly unable to forget her son." She goes on:

> Your father probably thinks that your mother is gone from this world. Do not tell him that I have spoken to you of her. Know in your heart that she is alive, and come to see me as the occasion allows. I will arrange for you to meet her in secret. (p. 235)

The boy is deeply moved and upon his return home says to his wet nurse, "I saw someone who I believe to be my mother."

Astonished his wet nurse asks, "Where is she? How do you know she is your mother? What did she look like?" With deep emotion the boy describes his mother's charm, her noble beauty, but says he must not tell his father because his mother has forbidden him. Even a boy knows how to keep a secret.

Chûjô marries the second daughter of the Prince of Yoshino and is able to find happiness, but to the end he fails to understand why Sister disappears, leaving her child behind. He seeks help from his new wife who seemingly knows some important facts about Sister's disappearance, but he desists from pursuing the matter when he fails to get any clear answers. It is important to know when to stop. Chûjô sacrifices his desire to know and saves his own and his family's happiness. This also reflects the absence of jealousy.

Some of you may not agree with Chûjô or the Emperor. They pursue their inquiry only up to a certain point. It may seem important to know the whole truth no matter how painful it might be. I cannot say what is good or bad, but if I were to take the side of the author, I might say that jealousy is a dissonance in the overall harmony of love. Aesthetically speaking, harmony must not be interrupted by too much dissonance; on the other hand, a certain amount of dissonance enhances the overall beauty. For the author of *Torikaebaya* the most important thing is beauty.

4. Beauty

This story was strongly censured for its "immorality." I feel that the author's intent was neither to write a tale spiced with love scenes nor to concern himself with ethical issues; what he aimed for above all else was beauty. People of the time all knew the *Genji monogatari* (Tale of Genji) in which love scenes are depicted delicately and with profound insight into human nature. Perhaps the author of *Torikaebaya* sought to create an even greater beauty by endowing his characters with the virtue of both sexes. By incorporating love scenes secretly played out by two men with one in the role of a woman, and by two women with one in the role of a man, he was perhaps trying to show that a man is most beautiful when his femininity is revealed, and a woman most beautiful when her masculinity shines forth. The following episode illustrates this.

Sister receives a letter from a woman in the Reikeiden Hall. "He" goes there to linger in one of the narrow corridors illuminated by the late night moon; the two meet, talk, and exchange poems. But several months later Sister becomes pregnant and thinks of committing suicide. "He" then remembers the woman from Reikeiden.

I now quote the English translation:

When the courtiers and everyone else had gone to sleep, "he" [Sister] stealthily approached the Reikeiden.

Where did it go,
The moon I saw in winter?
I know not,
So very dark is it
On this hazy spring night.

Just as "he" charmingly recited the last line, someone drew near.

...
The moon slipped away from sight
I too knew not where;
Regretfully I wondered,
Had it forever vanished into the mountain?

From the response "he" realized it was the same lady "he" had known before. In "his" desolation, "he" had walked on without going specially to see her. "He" had assumed she would not remember "him" very well. But her feelings for "him" had not changed. As a result, "he" found it hard to go on his own way, and "he" approached her. (p. 107-8)

Sister's love for the woman from the Reikeiden is an allusion to Genji's love for Hanachirusato in *The Tale of Genji*. Hanachirusato likewise makes her appearance to console Genji when he is deeply disappointed. The author of *Torikaebaya* recreates the scene, but this time with two women, one in the role of a man. By doing so the emotion is intensified and surpasses the aesthetic pathos of *Genji*.

Here is another example. Sister decides to go to Uji following Chûjô's suggestion that she deliver her child there in secret.

On the way to Uji "he" [Sister] was overcome with gloom, wondering why this had happened to "him." The moon rose clear, and the scenery along the road was beautiful. When they reached Kohata, an area of lowly mountain folk who would not notice anything unusual about them, "he" threw off "his" reserve, revealing her female self. She had with her only the flute she had been attached to since childhood. To part from it would have grieved her above all else in the world. Depressed as she was, she played beautifully, the sounds quite indescribable.

This scene also alludes to *Genji,* in which two lovers likewise escape to Uji. The most striking difference between the parallel episodes is that while there are scenes in which young men play the flute in *Genji,* Sister plays the flute in *Torikaebaya,* an instrument usually reserved for men. Here the beauty is heightened as we see the young woman play the flute in that unique moment of transition between manhood and womanhood. She would never play the flute again. The pathos of her situation captured in a singular instant of eternity heightens our aesthetic awareness.

There are many other love scenes enacted by two men or two women which do not allude to *Genji.* The author no doubt felt that he had discovered a highly effective means of rendering beauty. Once when Chûjô is impressed by Sister in her male role, he compares her to a cherry blossom, a common metaphor for female beauty. He must have subconsciously sensed the presence of femininity. The alternating yet simultaneous presence of the masculine and feminine serve to bring each other into relief in a most sublime fashion. Like the brilliance of the moon against the backdrop of the night which captures our attention more than the light of the sun, or the male Kabuki actor who achieves a femininity unattainable by women, we are made to sense the presence of the masculine and feminine in a new and powerful way.

Through his ingenuity the author of *Torikaebaya* opens up new vistas of beauty which had been thought to be completed by *The Tale of Genji*.

5. Locus

The locus of action in *Torikaebaya is* also significant. There are three main locales: Kyoto, Uji and Yoshino. Uji is located just outside of Kyoto to the south. One can walk there from Kyoto in a few hours. Yoshino is located farther south, and it takes a whole day to make the trek on foot. I have prepared a chart of the locus of the three main characters, Brother, Sister, and Chûjô, which immediately reveals some interesting facts (see Figure 11).

Chûjô is very active, especially in the first half of the story, but as the chart shows, his actions are limited to Kyoto and Uji, and he knows nothing of what happens in Yoshino. Sister goes there when she becomes pregnant, and Brother visits there when he takes the role of a man; they are both made to reveal their true nature. The most important encounter between Sister and Brother, when the latter arrives to take the former to Yoshino, takes place in Uji while Chûjô is in Kyoto. Chûjô knows nothing about this although he often makes trips to Uji.

The crucial exchange of roles between Brother and Sister takes place in Yoshino. Only the Prince who is aware of everything knows about their secret. He even knows their destiny and foresees that Sister will become Empress and that Brother will attain the highest position in court. The only thing of which the Prince is uncertain is his daughters' destiny. He has a hunch that Sister will take them to Kyoto and asks her about this. At this point he is just an anxious father who only wishes for his daughters' happiness.

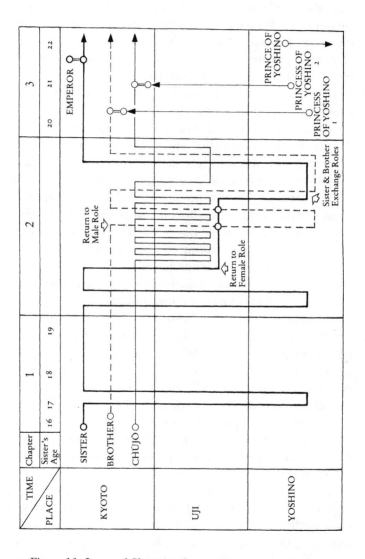

Figure 11. Locus of Changing Sexual Roles in Torikaebaya

One cannot know everything as long as one is tied to this world. When his daughters are taken to Kyoto by Brother, the Prince promises the latter that there is nothing to worry about. Everything goes smoothly and his daughters are fulfilled. The Prince then disappears deep into the mountains of Yoshino. He no longer "lives in this world." One cannot maintain one's ties to this world when everything including destiny is known.

During her extended absence Sister's father becomes deeply depressed. Brother meanwhile takes the role of a man to go on a search for his Sister. The father has a dream in which a noble priest appears and tells him that his children's roles had been reversed due to transgressions committed in their former lives but that the time had come for them to be liberated. The father is delighted and tells his wife about the dream, whereupon the latter tells him that Brother has already become a man and gone out in search of Sister. Here we have a beautiful concordance between inner and outer reality, the dream in Kyoto and the event in Yoshino.

Dreams in *Torikaebaya*, however, do not always have such a deep significance. When Sister first thinks *of* going to Yoshino, "he" tells "his" family and the people of the court that as "he" has had some bad dreams "he" is going to visit a temple in the mountains to purify "himself." This shows that the people of the time both respected dreams as divine oracles and were able to use them to their own ends when necessary, even when they did not actually have any.

The following episode demonstrates yet another use of dreams. After Sister and Brother exchange roles, Sister goes as "Brother" (who is believed to be a woman) to the palace of the Crown Princess after "a long absence." No one doubts that she is anyone but "Brother" (i.e. Sister's "sister"). One of the attendants tells her of the former's fears that the Princess might be pregnant and asks Sister if she knows who the man is. If anyone should know, it would be "Brother" since "she" is the Princess's closest attendant.

Sister carefully answers that she felt something to be wrong but never suspected that the Princess was pregnant. She goes on to explain that she had to return home due to her brother's disappearance, and that she had to stay there because she had fallen ill. When she recovered she received a secret letter from her brother stating that he had a strange dream in which the Crown Princess has become pregnant. That Sister returned to the palace at her brother's urging.

The attendant is satisfied with this explanation and is silently convinced that the man who made the Princess pregnant must have been Sister's brother. Without saying a word about the possible identity of the man, Sister thus succeeds in convincing the attendant that the former had secretly arranged a love affair between the Princess and Sister's brother. It was in fact Brother (in his previous role as a woman) who had made the Princess pregnant. Once again a dream is used to avoid unnecessary disturbance, but with even greater subtlety than before.

We have just seen three levels at which dreams are dealt with in *Torikaebaya*. Sister's father, the Minister of the Left, has a dream at the deepest level where it conveys a meaningful truth to him. Sister uses a dream she has not had as an excuse for going to Yoshino is bound to the intentions of consciousness. Sister's second use of the dream is more subtle as she succeeds in tacitly conveying false information in order to relate the truth. These three levels correspond remarkably well to the three main loci of action. The dream seen by the Minister of the Left is directly concerned with events in Yoshino. Sister's use of the dream as an excuse is aimed at avoiding trouble in

Kyoto. Sister's other dream is also consciously fabricated but works at the subconscious level to hide the exchange of roles between Sister and Brother in Yoshino. It is noteworthy that the Japanese of that time had a highly differentiated understanding of the manner in which dreams could be dealt with.

6. Ego and Psyche

The chart of the loci of the main characters in Figure 11 locates Sister, Brother, and Chûjô as they move between Kyoto, Uji, and Yoshino. The manner in which they move and their corresponding actions calls to mind Jung's categories of "consciousness," "the personal unconscious," and "the collective unconscious." Stories involving sex role interchange, like fairy tales, have been interpreted by Jungians as revealing aspects of the individuation process. My feeling regarding these interpretations is that they have been made primarily from the standpoint of the ego. That is, the various processes involved were seen in terms of the establishment of the ego and its efforts to regain contact with the deeper layers of the unconscious.

A similar approach may be tried with *Torikaebaya.* But who represents the ego: Sister, Brother, or Chûjô? And where is the dragon fight which establishes the hero as the center of consciousness? There is no central conflict in this story, although there are many figures who struggle to find a life which they can call their own. Perhaps it would be better not to see this story in terms of the ego-standpoint.

If one were to insist on locating the ego, however, I would say that Chûjô is the most suitable candidate. He is handsome, able and loved by many women. He has an affair with Sister's wife and learns that they had not had any sexual relations. He moreover has an affair with Sister and even succeeds in removing her from her house and having her secretly moved to Uji. He thus far seems to be a capable figure, able to take the role of the ego. However, when Sister suddenly disappears he is at a complete loss. Yet in the end he marries a beautiful princess and attains happiness.

But rather than bring the story to a close here, the author goes on to talk about Chûjô's feelings of sadness over the disappearance of his beloved, Sister:

> What were her feelings when she resigned herself neither to see nor to know her son and to go into eternal seclusion? he wondered.
>
> I am told that he [Chûjô] felt sorrow, pain, and longing, and was overcome with grief.

I found this ending, which speaks of Chûjô's sorrow and wonder, quite compelling. At first it seems he can control everything. But with Sister's mysterious disappearance he is made to know that there are things he cannot understand. Even though he is able to connect with the princess from Yoshino, who represents the deeper layers of the psyche, he still has to suffer. I am tempted to call Chûjô the perfect caricature of the modern ego made to suffer through its own arrogance.

What about Brother, one might ask. At first he is weak, like a woman. But he establishes his masculinity later on as he helps his sister to escape from Uji and become a complete woman. In the end he marries the daughter of the Prince of Yoshino and attains his goal. Yet he does not engage in any fights along the way; the relationship with the princess is moreover established by Sister. It may be said that Brother's ego is fostered by the help of Sister who long endures and endeavors as a man. When seen in this light it may be better to speak of Sister and Brother as two aspects of one being rather than separate individuals. But can the ego be sometimes male and sometimes female? I think that the Brother-Sister pair forms an important component of the psyche but not the ego in the ordinary sense. The fact that they so closely resemble each other that they can exchange roles means that they are of one being, but the identity of this being is difficult to pin down. The activity of these two figures constitutes the basic plot as they move between Kyoto and Yoshino. Although they do not fight with others, they must endure great suffering to attain their goal.

There are a number of phenomena in the psyche which can be elucidated in a most illuminating manner in terms of this Female-Male being. Some may object that this being is inconsistent, as it shifts sex roles and fails to attain a logical unity. It is my feeling, however, that it is more desirable for a model of the psyche to achieve concordance with the actual workings of the psyche than to achieve logical consistency.

Let us look at the locus of action in *Torikaebaya* as a map of the psyche divided into three areas. Kyoto corresponds to consciousness, but it is interesting to note that there is enough room to conceal the Crown Princess's pregnancy which remains a secret to all but a few. Sometimes two people who are otherwise quite intimate do not share a secret with each other. Our consciousness is like this. We may know many things, but the contents of our knowledge are not always well connected. The connection is sometimes obstructed by complexes which in the story appear as events in Uji. The most important secret is located in Yoshino, the deepest layer of the collective unconscious, and is only accessible to the chosen few. Although some figures from Yoshino, namely the Prince's daughters, play important roles in the Kyoto area, the omniscient Prince cannot remain in this world and disappears into the mountains.

All of the events in this story can be interpreted from many different viewpoints: that of Chûjô, the Minister of the Left, Brother, or Sister. Each provides a different perspective, and as no one has a complete, "objective" view, there is inevitably some ambiguity. The only one who knows everything, the Prince of Yoshino, is gone.It is virtually impossible to understand the story from the standpoint of the ego for the story is itself a landscape of the psyche (see Figure 12).

Mozart is said to have stated that he could hear his entire symphony in a moment. He composed his symphonies to last twenty or thirty minutes so that he could make ordinary people understand what he heard in an instant. Perhaps *Torikaebaya* can be understood as a Mozart symphony. Although it takes hours to read, the entire story can be understood as one sublime moment, a beautiful description of the psyche consisting of innumerable concordances.

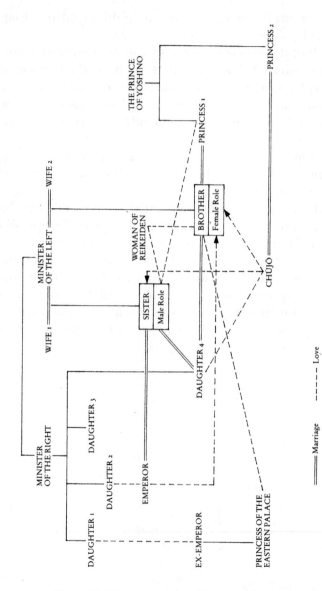

Figure 12. Viewpoints in the Torikaebaya Story

Appendix

The Changelings:
A summary of the Torikaebaya monogatari

Book One

Once there was a Minister of the Left who had two children, a boy and a girl, born to him of his two wives. They were beautiful and charming but showed a troubling inclination from early on. Brother was very shy and tended to play with dolls by himself, while Sister was rather outgoing, playing kickball and shooting arrows with boys outside. It grieved the Minister of the Left to know that his otherwise darling children should have such unusual natures.

The Minister of the Left had an older brother, the Minister of the Right, who had four daughters, and although the oldest one was the Emperor's concubine, the Emperor appointed his only daughter the Crown Princess of the Eastern Palace upon his retirement, and the Minister of the Right was left disappointed. He decided to take Sister as his youngest daughter's husband because the former was so handsome and seemed promising. Sister continued to rise in rank as expected and "his" father-in-law was very pleased, but "he" had a strange affliction which made it necessary for "him" to retire to the village of "his" wet nurse four or five days out of the month. As "he" took his monthly leave he would say, "I am afflicted by evil spirits. "

In the meantime Brother was appointed to the Eastern Palace as one of the Crown Princess's female attendants.

The two grew close, and to the Crown Princess's great surprise, Brother, who was supposed to be a woman, became physically intimate with her. This was kept a close secret. The new appointment also put Brother in close proximity to Sister, and they became closer, bonded in compassion for one another's plight.

There was a young man, Chûjô, a handsome lad who spent his time mingling with the ladies of the court who in turn lavished him with affection. He enjoyed a close fraternity with Sister, but Chûjô was in love with Sister's wife, the youngest daughter of the Minister of the Right. Although Sister was in every way an ideal companion and the couple had grown close in their wedded relationship, they of course lacked the physical bond. The young wife suffered, for she did not know the cause of this lack and blamed herself. Chûjô knew of this and, unable to hold himself back, forced himself upon her and made her pregnant. Although Sister was unaware of this new development, she, too, suffered from her plight and increasingly engaged in religious austerities to assuage her emotions.

Just about this time a prince returned from his studies in China. He excelled in all things: scholarly pursuits, divination, astronomy, dream interpretation, and physiognomy. He had taken a Chinese wife who had borne him two daughters, but she had died shortly after giving birth, and as he had begun to feel increasingly isolated, he returned to Japan. But after such a long absence the people of his land suspected him of scheming to become the sovereign, and in order to avoid persecution, he took the tonsure and retired into the mountains of Yoshino.

Sister, too, had been dwelling more and more on the thought of leaving this world. Hearing of the Prince of Yoshino she wrote to ask if she might visit him. He wrote back to her giving her permission, and in order to keep a low profile Sister told people:

> Someone interpreted my dreams as very disturbing and said that I ought to stay at a mountain temple for a week or so to have purification services held. I feel restless when my whereabouts are known, and people coming to see me would distract me.... (p. 61)

The Prince had been worried about the fate of his daughters, but when he met Sister he knew that he had found the one who would take care of them. Sister in turn intimated her grief, and the Prince was able to infer the true source of the problem. He told her:

> It won't last for long. Everything that has occurred is the result of events in your former lives and not in this one. You should, in any case, endure the circumstances of this life. It would be very childish and completely lacking in understanding for you to lament and resent others.... I believe that you are destined to attain a high position ... there will come a time when you will realize the import of my words. (p. 63)

Sister thanked the Prince and assured him that his daughters would be taken care of. She stayed in Yoshino for awhile and grew very close to the Prince's oldest daughter. The Princess had never been with such a charming "man" and the two exchanged intimacies throughout the night. Sister left for Kyoto vowing to return.

Both the Minister of the Left and Right and the latter's daughter, Sister's "wife," were miserable during "his" absence. The Minister of the Right's daughter had increasingly taken solace in Chûjô's companionship, and when Sister returned "he" found that "his" wife, "was, for some reason, unfeeling; yet it was futile to reproach her."

Sister continued to make visits to Yoshino; in the meantime a daughter was born to "his" wife, and Sister increasingly suspected that the culprit was Chûjô whom the baby so closely resembled.

Chûjô had always wondered why Sister and "his" wife had not been intimate, but he still did not understand the reason. There was a great celebration for the newborn baby, and Sister discovered that Chûjô had visited "his" wife during this time at a high risk of exposure; Sister "might have been resentful, but 'he' did not feel so jealous." "He" felt it natural for Chûjô to behave in this way, but lamented "his" wife's lack of care and took this as a sign of her affection for Chûjô.

Chûjô could never be satisfied with one woman. He had always admired Brother (who had grown up to be a beautiful woman) and approached "her," but he was coldly turned away. Dejected, he went to cry on the shoulder of his friend from childhood, Sister, who embraced him to give him comfort. Chûjô returned the embrace and discovered the truth; now he had to have Sister, the most beautiful of all. Sister, horrified, refused to see Chûjô on the pretext of being ill, but the two eventually met when Sister unavoidably made an appearance in the imperial court. Chûjô found an opportunity to be alone with Sister, and seeing the former's uncontrollable emotion, Sister felt sorry for him as a pitiful nuisance. Sister tried to avoid him, but Chûjô would not leave her alone and went to her quarters at night during one of her trips to her wet nurse's village:

> Darkness envelops me,
> Descending from clouds and grief.
> Tears and autumn rain fall.
> Though wet am I, had I not come
> How might I have seen you?

... He left nothing unsaid. Since there was no need for him to feel any reticence in this secluded place, [Chûjô] had lain down on top of [Sister], and weeping and laughing, they spoke of many things. One could never repeat it all. (p. 92)

Chûjô wished to hide Sister away somewhere and make her all his own. Sister, on the other hand, lamenting Chûjô's fickle heart and the uncertainty of the human world in general, dwelled on the thought of becoming a nun. "His" wife had been increasingly betraying her love for Chûjô, and Sister lingered near the Reikeiden Hall where "he" had heard the voice of a woman who had previously expressed her admiration for Sister (as a desirable man):

> Where did it go,
> The moon I saw in winter?
> I know not,
> So very dark is it
> On this hazy spring night.

Just as [Sister] charmingly recited the last line someone drew near.

> As I gazed at it,
> The moon slipped away from sight,
> I too knew not where;
> Regretfully I wondered,
> Had it forever vanished into the mountain?

From the response "he" realized it was the same lady "he" had known before. (pp. 107-8)

"He" was so desolate that "he" sought comfort anywhere, but of course this stranger could not resolve his suffering.

Book Two

In order to avoid further embarrassment Sister accepted Chûjô's offer to take refuge in the residence of the
latter's uncle in Uji. Sister quietly took leave of "his" wife,
made a brief visit to Brother, and left Kyoto with a few of
"his" closest attendants without letting anyone know why
or where.

> On the way to Uji [Sister] was overcome with gloom, won-
> dering why this had happened to "him." The moon rose
> clear, and the scenery along the road was beautiful. When
> they reached Kohata, an area of lowly mountain folk who
> would not notice anything unusual about them, [Sister]
> threw off "his" reserve, [and revealed her female self]. She
> had with her only the flute she had been attached to since
> childhood.... Depressed as she was, she played beautifully,
> the sounds quite indescribable. (p. 116)

Everyone in Kyoto lamented Sister's disappearance
and began to suspect from the baby's appearance that an
affair had taken place between Chûjô and the daughter
of the Minister of the Right. When it became clear that
this was in fact the case, the Minister was infuriated and
disowned his daughter. She became more miserable than
ever and increasingly withdrawn.

Brother was anxious about Sister's disappearance and
the general commotion made him unsettled. He decided
to go in search of his Sister and dressed as a man:

> Then, putting on a hunting robe and trousers over "her"
> clothes, "she" summoned one of "her" wet nurse's children,
> an assistant of the Imperial Princess's, to come behind "her"
> curtains and cut "her" hair.... He [now] looked exactly like
> the missing [Sister had before]. (p. 129)

Brother knew that his Sister had been visiting the
Prince of Yoshino and headed out to see the Prince. Stop-

ping in Uji for a rest, the two saw each other for a moment. But as they had exchanged their roles, they failed to recognize each other. When Brother reached Yoshino, the Prince told him that he should have word soon concerning Sister and predicted she would someday become the Empress Dowager. Chûjô had made Sister's "wife" pregnant once again, and Sister was distressed as the former ran back and forth between Kyoto and Uji, but Sister "was not so frail and gloomy as a woman would normally be."

> Because her heart was experienced in the ways of the world, even when she worried and grieved she was not so completely overcome as a woman ordinarily would be. When she had to weep she would, and when something amusing was said she would smile. (p. 139)

Sister sent word to the Prince of Yoshino as she had promised, and when the Prince read the letter to Brother, the latter realized that the woman he had seen in Uji was his Sister. Overjoyed, he wrote to Sister immediately, and the two met in Uji. Meanwhile Chûjô was with the youngest daughter of the Minister of the Right to oversee the delivery of her second child.

Brother returned to Kyoto for a brief visit, determined to go to Uji again to be with his Sister. The night of his return to the capital his father had a dream:

> A priest, worthy of respect and pure, came to him and said: "Do not grieve so! The affairs of both [Sister] and [Brother] are settled. In the morning when it grows light you will learn of their circumstances. In previous lives their paths were crossed, and in retribution a goblin changed [their sexual identities] ... and caused you no end of sorrow.... As a result of your having entered on the path of the Buddha, ... the situation has been completely remedied.

The man will be a man, and the woman a woman, and they will be made to prosper as you wish.... (p. 149)

Brother, now a splendid man, told his father that Sister, too, had returned to her original nature as a woman. Asking that his father keep this matter a secret, Brother left for Uji. While waiting for Brother, Sister also resolved to leave Uji, but was worried about leaving her child behind. Nevertheless she thought:

"Since the bond between parent and child is so deeply rooted, we are sure to cross paths again. No matter how dear my baby may be to me, how can I, once so celebrated in society, go on passing the days in waiting for one man to pay me an occasional visit in this desolate place?" (p. 151)

Upon Brother's arrival, the two departed for Yoshino. At the palace of the Prince of Yoshino Brother quickly learned the ways and arts of a man becoming to Sister's previous position. Sister had already been transformed into a beautiful woman. The two could not stay in Yoshino forever, so they returned to the capital, Brother as a man and Sister as a woman.

No one knew of Brother's disappearance except the Princess of the Eastern Palace and her closest attendants, and Sister's absence was blamed on the affair involving Chûjô and the Minister's daughter. Brother was welcomed back into the imperial court; he reconciled his (i.e. originally Sister's) relationship with his wife. She was surprised and confused, especially at the sudden awakening of the sexual impulse in her husband, but she was nonetheless rescued from her state of languor.

Chûjô was preoccupied with his new baby, but he also longed for Sister and returned to the capital. It never crossed his mind that the two had exchanged roles when he saw Brother carrying out the former role of Sister.

Chûjô, who was always so busy in pursuing and looking after his love affairs, never realized the truth.

Book Three

The Princess of the Eastern Palace had become pregnant, and Sister told the Princess's attendants that she had been away for so long because she had fallen ill during her search for her brother:

> I was very anxious about the Princess, but too depressed even to write.... When my uneasiness began to slacken I was anxious to return at once. 'I had a dream that revealed to me that the Princess was possibly pregnant, [my brother] secretly told me at the time, 'but I've not been able to determine whether this is true or not'.... It was then that I understood the Princess's condition. (p. 180)

All of this led the attendant to believe that it was Sister's Brother (who had originally been the sister) who was the one responsible for the Princess's pregnancy. This was the truth, of course, ingeniously planted in the mind of the attendant.

The ex-Emperor had been worried about the Princess's "strange illness," and when she had her child it became safe to have her transferred to her father's palace. Brother's family was told about the baby, and they received their newborn grandson into their family with great joy.

The Emperor had longed for Sister all his life; he now learned that she had "matured" out of her "shyness and fragile condition," and he could not wait to see her. He forced himself upon her and suddenly realized that she was not a virgin. Though he now thought he understood why the Minister of the Left had kept him away from his daughter – there had been some terrible love affair – he did not care about what had happened in the past and did not wish to probe the matter too deeply. The two were eventually united in public and Sister became the Empress; everyone was delighted.

Brother in the meantime had been preparing for the arrival of the daughter of the Prince of Yoshino and had a mansion built; both daughters were moved into the mansion as Sister had promised to take care of them. The Prince was also offered a lavish estate, but he explained that he had remained near the capital only out of his concern for his daughters, and refused the kind offer. He departed into the mountains to fulfill his longing for the religious life, and he was never seen again.

Chûjô was continually rebuffed in his attempts to approach Brother (whom he still thought to be Sister) and began to think about the youngest daughter of the Minister of the Right again. When he inquired after her, her attendant told him that she was to have Brother's child and would not see him. Chûjô was as confused as ever.

In time, however, perhaps realizing his past folly and now in possession of a child to care for, Chûjô became more settled, and Brother considered him as a possible husband for the younger daughter of the Prince of Yoshino. Chûjô and the young princess were brought together, and Brother was quite pleased. People were surprised that Brother could remain on such close terms with Chûjô after all that had happened, but Brother "had an excellent disposition; he thus acted differently than people in their incomplete understanding expected he would."

The youngest daughter of the Minister of the Left eventually gave birth to Brother's son, and Sister gave birth to an Imperial Prince; everyone was overjoyed. Several more children were born, among them Sister's daughter.

Sister, now the Empress, often had occasion to see her
son (the one born in Uji) who was in the custody of Chûjô
and his new wife, but was saddened by the silent gulf
which separated her from her son. One day her daughter
brought the boy to play in her palace. As she looked
closely into his eyes, tears flowed down her cheeks. It "occurred to the Uji boy that perhaps she was his mother,
and he was filled with emotion."
The boy lowered his head and felt his own tears fall.
The Empress said to him:

> I am a relative of your mother, and it pains me to see that
> she ... yearns for you, [seemingly unable to forget her son].
> This is why I spoke as I did.... Know in your heart that she is
> alive, and come to see me as the occasion allows. I will ar-
> range for you to meet her in secret. (p. 235)

The Uji boy returned to his wet nurse and said,

> I saw someone I think might be my mother.... Do not say
> anything though. She told me not to tell my father.... She
> was young and beautiful, more charming, more noble than
> Chûjô's wife, the younger Yoshino Princess. (p. 238)

The Emperor began to put the pieces of the puzzle
together and questioned Sister about Chûjô's oldest boy,
but when she appeared to be suffering from his prompt-
ings he desisted.
"The months and years passed and were replaced by
new ones." Everyone's children grew up to be more splendid than could be imagined, and there was prosperity
everywhere.

> Yet throughout all this ... never were [Chûjô's] sleeves dry
> of the bitter tears shed over the affair of the waves of the Uji
> River....

"What were her feelings when she resigned herself neither to see nor to know her son and to go into eternal seclusion?" he wondered.

I am told that he felt sorrow, pain, and longing, and was overcome with grief. (p. 239)[1]

1. *Acknowledgment:* This summary of Torikaebaya monogatari is based upon and quotations that appear in the text are reprinted from: *The Changelings: A Classical Japanese Court Tale*, Translated, with an Introduction and Notes by Rosette F. Willig; with the permission of the publishers, Stanford University Press, © 1983 by the Board of Trustees of the Leland Stanford Junior University.

Index

ENGLISH PUBLICATIONS BY *DAIMON*

Susan Bach – *Life Paints its Own Span*
E.A. Bennet – *Meetings with Jung*
George Czuczka – *Imprints of the Future*
Heinrich Karl Fierz – *Jungian Psychiatry*
von Franz / Frey-Rohn / Jaffé – *What is Death?*
Liliane Frey-Rohn – *Friedrich Nietzsche*
Yael Haft – *Hands: Archetypal Chirology*
Siegmund Hurwitz – *Lilith, the first Eve*
Aniela Jaffé   – *The Myth of Meaning*
                   – *Was C.G. Jung a Mystic?*
                   – *From the Life und Work of C.G. Jung*
                   – *Death Dreams and Ghosts*
Verena Kast   – *A Time to Mourn*
                   – *Sisyphus*
James Kirsch   – *The Reluctant Prophet*
Rivkah Schärf Kluger   – *The Gilgamesh Epic*
Rafael López-Pedraza   – *Hermes and his Children*
                         – *Cultural Anxiety*
Alan McGlashan – *The Savage and Beautiful Country*
                   – *Gravity and Levity*
Gitta Mallasz (Transcription) – *Talking with Angels*
C.A. Meier   – *Healing Dream and Ritual*
                   – *A Testament to the Wilderness*
Laurens van der Post – *A «Festschrift»*
R.M. Rilke – *Duino Elegies*
Ann Ulanov – *The Wizards' Gate*

Jungian Congress Papers:
Jerusalem 1983 – *Symbolic and Clinical Approaches*
Berlin 1986 – *Archetype of Shadow in a Split World*
Paris 1989 – *Dynamics in Relationship*
Chicago 1992 – *The Transcendent Function*

Available from your bookstore or from our distributors:

In the United States:

Atrium Publishers Group
P.O. Box 108
Lower Lake, CA 95457
Tel. (707) 995 3906
Fax: (707) 995 1814

Chiron Publications
400 Linden Avenue
Wilmette, IL 60091
Tel. (708) 256 7551
Fax: (708) 256 2202

In Great Britain:

Airlift Book Company
26-28 Eden Grove
London N7 8EF, England
Tel. (607) 5792 and 5798
Fax (607) 6714

Worldwide: Daimon Verlag
                 Hauptstrasse 85
                 CH-8840 Einsiedeln Switzerland
                 Tel. (41)(55) 532266
                 Fax (41)(55) 532231   *Write for our complete catalog!*